About this Bo[ok]

This book takes you off the beaten track to explore a selection [...] and South Manchester area. It includes 13 cycling routes t[...] variety of locations around the region.

All the routes are circular (as illustrated on the map below), [...] on each route - and many of the routes touch (or come clos[...] [..]her routes, so you can ad-lib and interconnect sections to form your own routes as your gravel knowledge of the area grows.

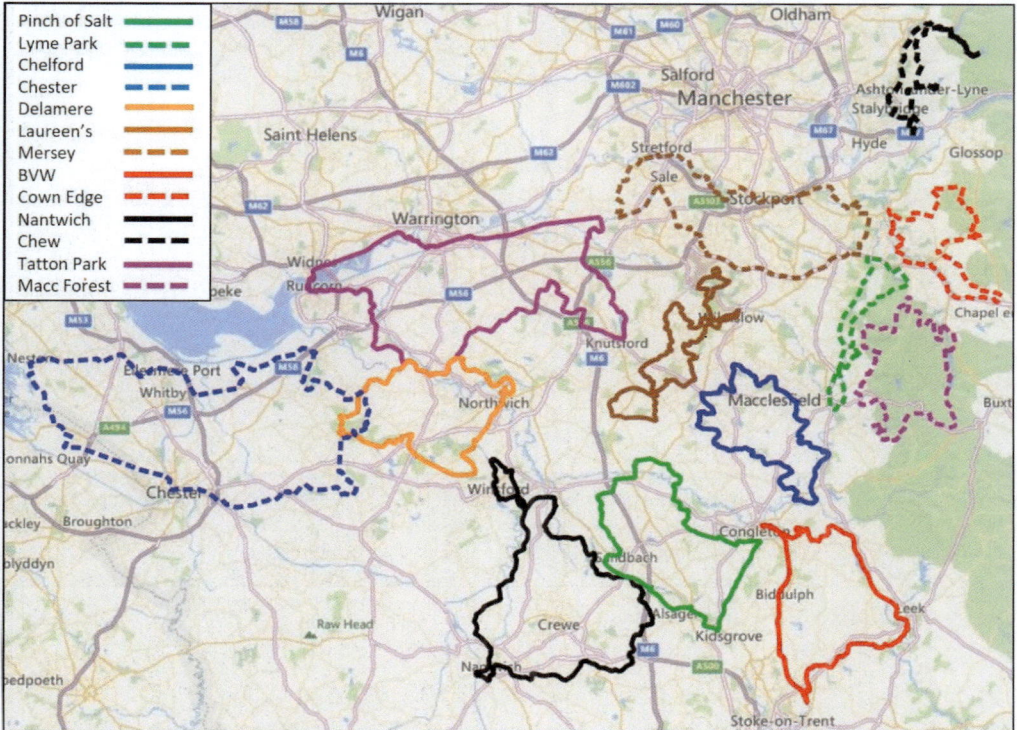

Pinch of Salt	
Lyme Park	
Chelford	
Chester	
Delamere	
Laureen's	
Mersey	
BVW	
Cown Edge	
Nantwich	
Chew	
Tatton Park	
Macc Forest	

Some of the highlights that you will encounte[r] on the routes include:

- Lyme Park
- Tatton Park
- Delamere Forest
- Macclesfield Forest
- The Goyt Valley
- The Biddulph Valley Way
- The Middlewood Way
- The Whitegate Way
- The Chester Millennium Greenway
- The Trans Pennine Trail
- Dovestone Reservoir
- … and sections along most of the canals in the area

All the routes have navigation files (.gpx format), which are available for free-download.

Contents

Disclaimer

This guide is not intended for the treatment or prevention of disease, nor as a substitute for medical treatment, nor as an alternative to medical advice. It is presented for information purposes only. Use of this guide is at the sole choice and risk of the reader. The author shall remain free of any fault, liability or responsibility for any loss or harm, whether real or perceived, resulting from the use of information in this guide.

The information provided within this guide is understood to be correct at the time of writing, the author cannot be held responsible for omissions, errors or subsequent changes.

Published by UK Cycle Routes 2020

https://ukcycleroutes.com/

All text, diagrams and photographs copyright © UK Cycle Routes

Acknowledgements

Maps contained within this publication have been created using QGIS

Maps © www.thunderforest.com, Data © www.osm.org/copyright

Elevation profiles of selected climbs have been created from Veloviewer.com

Hill ranking formula from climbbybike.com

Many thanks to John Wych, Nick Watkin, Lee Eaton, Neil Bradley & Russ Facer for their trust & patience in my route planning and persistence in seeking the answer to "I wonder where that track goes...?"

Cover Photos: Lee & Neil on the TPT along the Mersey (top); Macclesfield Forest (bottom)

INTRODUCTION

The basis for UK gravel riding typically includes one or more of four potential ingredients: former railway lines; canal towpaths; waymarked cycle routes; and individual sections of permissible track. The pros and cons of these are summarised below - more specific detail follows later in the book.

Former Railway Lines

The key aspects of old railway lines are that they are of shallow gradient and usually wide enough to allow for easy overtaking of walkers and avoiding oncoming cyclists (if they ride on the left!). Rural lines tend to have a surface of hard-packed gravel, enabling a good average speed, but can be prone to puddles. Lines in urban areas tend to be tarmacked, so great for off-road riding but obviously lacking the "gravel" dimension. If you are after more adventurous riding, then old railway lines are rather tame.

Canal Towpaths

With the exception of sections of the Bridgewater Canal, all the canals referenced in this book are managed by the Canal and River Trust, which permits cycling on towpaths (no permit required). The gradient is generally flat (apart from flights of locks) but the surface of the towpaths is highly variable. Some sections of canal are tarmacked, some are hard-packed gravel and some are vague grassy tracks - so do your research (and read the relevant chapter of this book) before you embark.

The canal network is extensive, so you can cover significant distances - I once rode a continuous 27km along a rural and bumpy section of the Trent and Mersey Canal - and felt pretty beaten-up afterwards!

Waymarked Cycle Routes

The Cheshire and South Manchester area is criss-crossed by over a dozen waymarked cycle routes. Some of the routes are all on-road, whilst others mix on-road with off-road. If you follow a section of one of these routes, you can be safe in the knowledge that it offers permissible cycling. Be prepared, though as some of the off-road sections can be quite technical in nature, especially Route 68.

Individual Sections of Permissible Tracks

Such sections include unadopted roads, byways open to all traffic (BOAT) and bridleways. There is a vast number of these tracks across the area covered by this book - many included in the routes.

These sections typically offer the most adventurous and exhilarating cycling but please be aware that there are many bridleways that are steep and rocky - and thus more suitable for mountain biking rather than gravel biking (depending on your aptitude and appetite!).

For a complete catalogue of the trails more suitable for mountain biking (and therefore to potentially avoid on your gravel bike!), refer to my guide book on the subject.

Available from:

https://ukcycleroutes.com/

https://www.amazon.co.uk/Dave-Peart/e/B07H2PJCKM

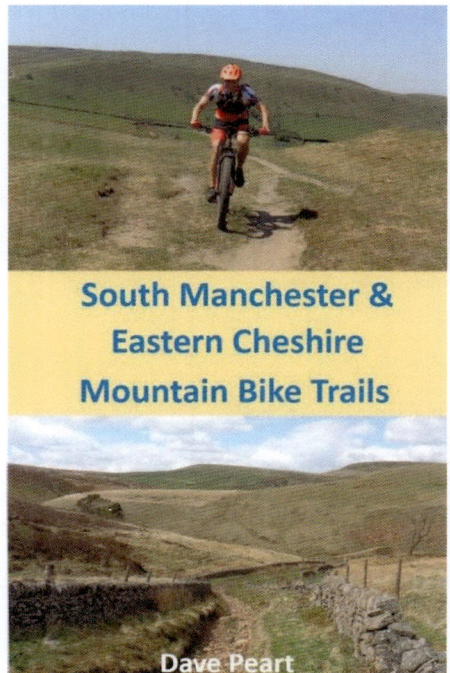

South Manchester & Eastern Cheshire Mountain Bike Trails

Dave Peart

Former Railway Lines

There are 18 former railways/tramways in the vicinity to consider for gravel rides, as described below.

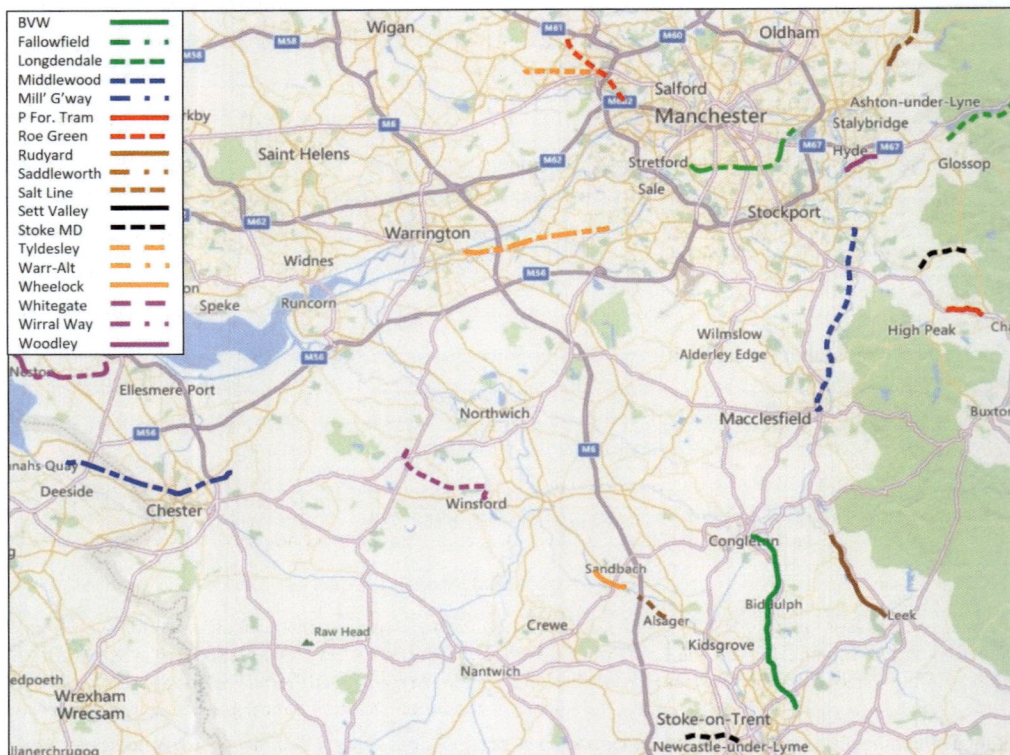

Line	From	To	Length	Notes
Biddulph Valley Way	Congleton	Stoke	17km	Hard-packed gravel
Fallowfield Loop	Chorlton	Audenshaw	11km	Tarmacked
Longdendale Trail	Padfield	Crowden	10km	Hard-packed gravel
Middlewood Way	Marple	Macclesfield	16km	Mainly hard-packed gravel
Millennium Greenway (Chester)	Shotton	Guilden Sutton	14km	Tarmacked
Peak Forest Tramway	Buxworth	Chapel Milton	3km	Stony track
Roe Green Loopline	Worsley	Farnworth	7km	Tarmacked, improved in 2016
Rudyard Lake	Leek	Rushton	8km	Hard-packed gravel
Saddleworth Linear	Saddleworth	Mossley	5km	Mix of tarmac and gravel
The Salt Line	Alsager	Hassall Green	2.5km	Hard-packed gravel
Sett Valley Way	Hayfield	New Mills	4km	Hard-packed gravel
Stoke to Market Drayton	Stoke	M. Drayton	4km	Tarmacked
Tyldesley Loop Line	Tyldesley	Worsley	6km	Tarmacked, improved in 2017
Warrington to Altrincham Line	Thelwall	Altrincham	12km	Hard-packed gravel
Wheelock Rail Trail	Malkins Bank	Ettiley Heath	3km	Hard-packed gravel
Whitegate Way	Winsford	Cuddington	10km	Hard-packed gravel
Wirral Way	Hooton	West Kirby	19km	Mix of tarmac and gravel
Woodley - Hattersley Link	Woodley	Hattersley	2.5km	Tarmacked

Canal Towpaths

There are 15 canals in the vicinity to consider for gravel rides, as described below.

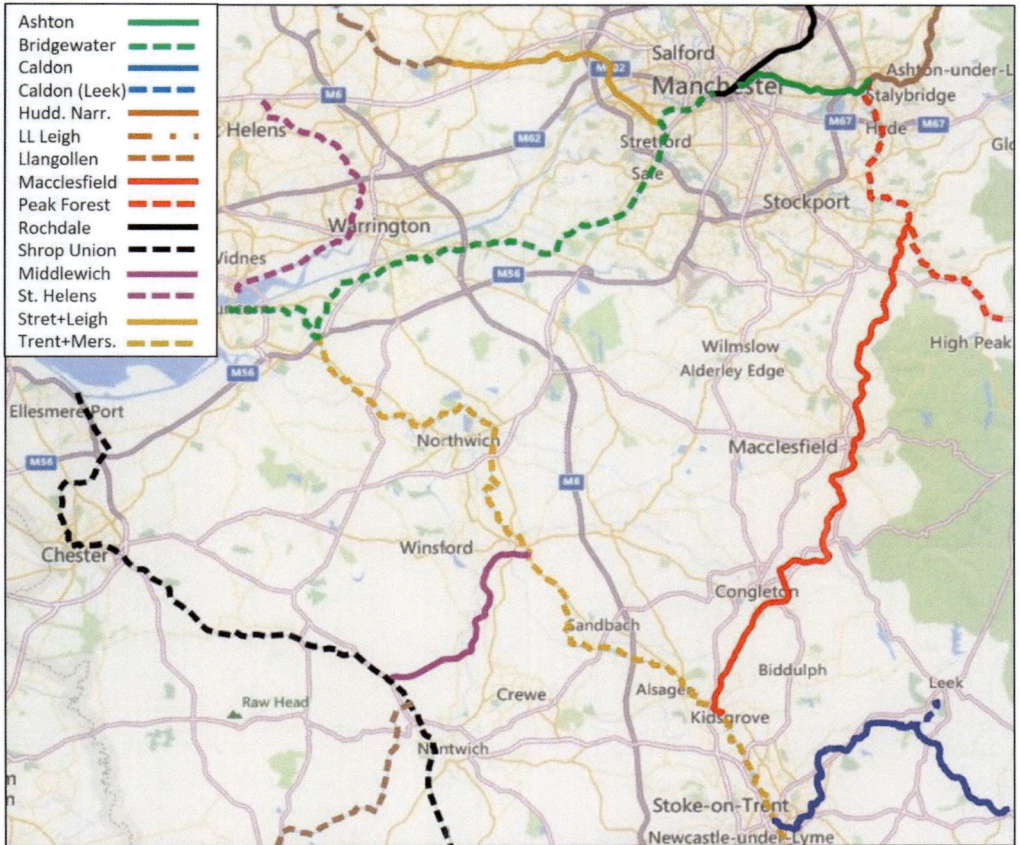

Canal	From	To	Length	Notes
Ashton Canal	Manchester	Ashton	10km	Hard-packed gravel, some cobbles
Bridgewater Canal (BWC)	Manchester	Runcorn	45km	Not permissible for whole length www.bridgewatercanal.co.uk
Caldon Canal	Stoke	Froghall	27km	Follows Cycle Route 550
Caldon Canal (Leek Branch)	Leek	Hazelhurst	5km	Follows Cycle Route 559
Huddersfield Narrow Canal	Huddersfield	Ashton	34km	Includes 2 (non-cycling) tunnels
Leeds & L'pool (Leigh Branch)	Leigh	Wigan	11km	Generally good surface
Llangollen Canal (SUC)	Llangollen	Hurleston	74km	Rural canal - mixed surface
Macclesfield Canal	Marple	Kidsgrove	44km	Rural canal - mixed surface
Peak Forest Canal	Ashton	Buxworth	24km	Generally good surface
Rochdale Canal	Manchester	Halifax	52km	Hard-packed gravel, some cobbles
Shropshire Union Canal (SUC)	Ellesmere Port	Oxley	107km	Good surface near towns, mixed otherwise
Middlewich Branch (SUC)	Middlewich	Wardle	16km	Rural canal - mixed surface
St. Helens (Sankey) Canal	St. Helens	Widnes	24km	Cycle route for most of its length
Stretford & Leigh Branch (BWC)	Stretford	Leigh	17km	Cycle route for most of its length
Trent & Mersey Canal	Sawley Cut	Preston (OTH)	152km	Rural canal - mixed surface

Waymarked Cycle Routes

There are 5 notable waymarked routes to consider for gravel rides, as described below.

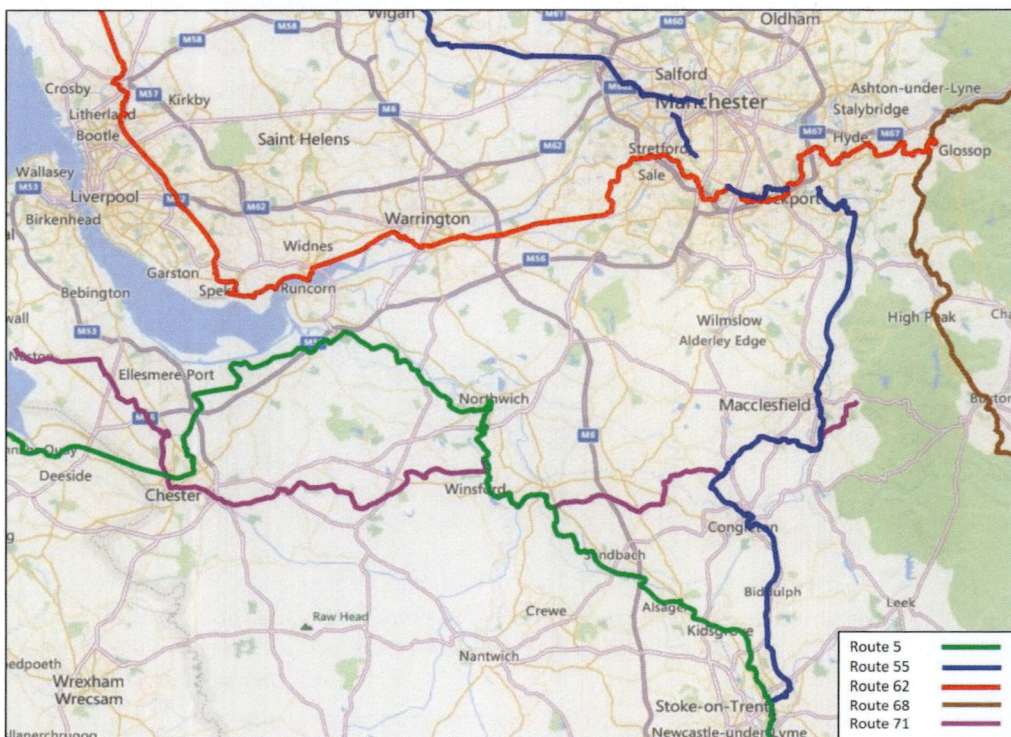

Route	From	To	Length	Notes
NCN Route 5	Reading	Holyhead	590km	Includes: The Salt Line and Wheelock Rail Trail, sections of the Trent & Mersey Canal and some of the Middlewich Branch of the Shropshire Union Canal
NCN Route 55	Ironbridge	Preston	182km	Currently has gaps to the north of Stockport. Includes: a section of the Trent and Mersey Canal, Biddulph Valley Way, Middlewood Way and the Roe Green and Tyldesley Looplines
NCN Route 62	Fleetwood	Selby	336km	Includes: St. Helens Canal, Warrington-Altrincham Line, the riverside path along the Mersey and the Longdendale Trail
NCN Route 68	Derby	Horham	427km	A very rural trail, includes the Longdendale Trail (coincides with Route 62 for that section)
Regional Route 71	Tegg's Nose	Neston	100km	A real mix of bridleways, also includes some of the Whitegate Way, plus sections of the Middlewich Branch and the main Shropshire Union Canal through Chester

What is a "Gravel Bike"? ...and which bike do I need to ride these routes?

There are two key questions to address in this section:

1) **What makes a bike a "Gravel Bike"?**
   This is a popular (and growing) genre of bikes, so it is helpful to understand the relevant features of such bikes if you are planning to buy or build one.

2) **What type of bike is most suitable for a particular gravel route?**
   The routes in this book span a wide range of terrain, ranging from relatively smooth and flat old railways to steep bridleways littered with rocks and loose stones. This section explains how different bike specifications align to the demands of the route terrain.

Gravel Bikes

The perfect gravel bike would pair the on-road speed of a road bike with the off-road capability of a mountain bike. In reality, it's how you strike the right balance for the key components. The image below shows a typical gravel bike.

Top of the list is **tyre choice** - more extreme terrain demands wider tyres with notable tread, which has a detrimental impact on rolling resistance - and hence your on-road speed. My recommendation is:

- 30-35mm tyres with a conservative tread pattern for general riding on hard-packed trails;
- 40-50mm tyres with a pronounced tread for more advanced riding (your frame and forks will dictate the maximum width of tyres that you can fit to your bike).

Other tyre factors to consider are:

- Tyre/wheel diameter - typically this will be 700c (same as a road bike), but some bikes will also accommodate smaller 650b (27.5" MTB) wheels with wider tyres;
- A tubeless setup (without an innertube, similar to a car tyre), which offers better puncture protection but does need tubeless-compatible wheels and tyres.

The next components to consider are the **brakes**.

-   Disc brakes are the norm for gravel bikes as they provide more effective braking than rim brakes, especially in wet and muddy conditions. They also avoid wearing out the wheel rims. If your budget can accommodate, then hydraulic brakes offer more powerful braking than cable-operated brakes.
-   Note also that rim brake callipers will limit the width of tyre that will fit.
-   Another option would be older-style cantilever or V-brakes, which will permit the use of wider tyres but still have the issue of rim-wear.

For **gears**, it will depend on the variety of terrain you intend to ride. There are two variations on specification.

-   A single chainring (termed "1x"), which follows the trend of mountain bikes - removing the complexity of a front derailleur, reducing instances of dropping the chain, but potentially reducing the range of gears (although very wide ratio cassettes address this issue).
-   Two (or three) chainrings, which give a wide range of gears but have a higher risk of dropping the chain and have more moving parts to fail or clog with dirt.

If your intended use is flatter and faster riding, then a double chainring system would be preferable. If you intend to ride more demanding terrain, then a 1x setup would be more advantageous.

Note that some bike frames have been designed to be 1x-specific (e.g. to provide maximum tyre clearance).

If you are considering a 1x setup, then look for a wide ratio cassette such as 11-42 (or wider) to give you a low enough bottom gear for steep climbs.

Typically, gravel bikes have drop **handlebars**, but in contrast to road bikes, they tend to be wider (to give you more leverage) and they flare out - the drops are wider than the tops to give your arms more clearance.

For **shoes and pedals**, the norm is to use a clipless setup, but choose one that will cope with mud. Taking Shimano as an example: choose SPD pedals (mountain bike 2-bolt standard) rather than SPD-SL (road bike 3-bolt standard), otherwise you won't be able to engage the cleats when you get muddy feet! (but you can ride with flat pedals if you don't feel confident being clipped-in on rough terrain)

Regarding **suspension**, most gravel bikes do not have any suspension features, however this trend is changing. Options for suspension include:

-   Suspension forks - usually with less travel than mountain bike forks (e.g. 60mm)
-   Compliant frames, whereby the frame is designed to flex vertically
-   Suspension stems - I personally use a Redshift stem that has 20mm of compliance and takes the sting out of small bumps and cobbles
-   Suspension seatposts, which offer either vertical travel or lateral flex

One final parameter to consider is **toe-overlap**, which is the gap (or overlap) between your forward shoe (with the pedals level) and the front tyre (or mudguard). This will depend on the frame size/geometry, crank length, cleat position, shoe size, tyre size and mudguard length. If the overlap is significant, it presents an accident risk if your shoe impedes the front tyre whilst steering (it can dislodge your shoe from the pedal or trap your shoe on the inside of the front wheel).

Which Bike is Best?

The answer to this question is: "it depends on the nature of the terrain you plan to ride". The diagram below shows a scale of 1 - 10 for the intensity of a section of terrain, whereby a rating of 1 refers to smooth tarmac and a rating of 10 refers to a highly technical section of trail littered with rocks (and typically steep and slippery!).

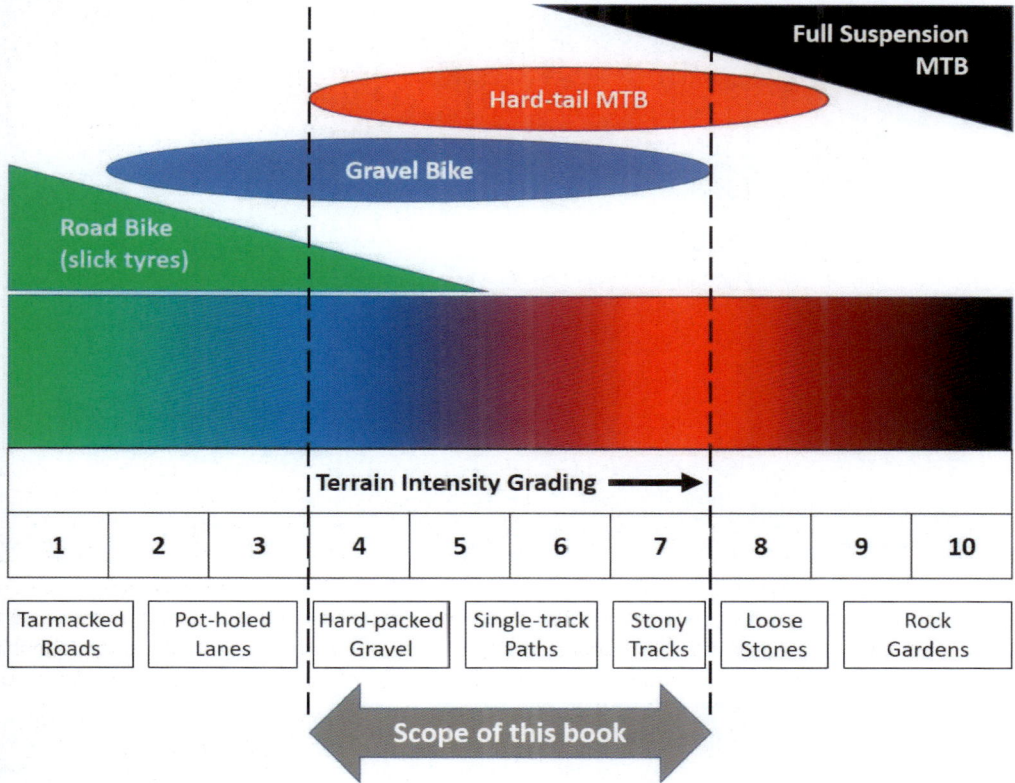

1	2	3	4	5	6	7	8	9	10
Tarmacked Roads	Pot-holed Lanes		Hard-packed Gravel	Single-track Paths		Stony Tracks	Loose Stones		Rock Gardens

Scope of this book

This book (and its collection of routes) is aimed at riding terrains in the range 4 -7 in the above diagram, all of which can be ridden on a drop-handlebar gravel bike. However, this is not the only bike you can use.

A mountain bike will better enable you to control the bike on stony tracks (sections with a rating of 7) but will not be as efficient to pedal on smoother sections as a gravel bike.

A hybrid bike is another option, which is essentially a less burly version of a hard-tail mountain bike; but it's suitability will depend on tyre selection (refer to the previous section), handlebar width and total weight of the bike.

Each of the routes in this book has a Terrain score (based on the above diagram) to help you decide on the choice of bike. Personally, I have a non-suspension gravel bike with 40mm tyres as well as a hard-tail mountain bike (with 2.3" tyres).

- For routes with ratings 5 and under, I will ride the gravel bike (faster & more efficient)
- For routes with ratings 7 and over, I will ride the mountain bike (better control)
- For routes with a rating of 6, I'll ride the gravel bike if the ground is dry and the mountain bike if it's wet/muddy.

INTRODUCING THE GRAVEL ROUTES

The table below summarises the 13 routes described in the book, along with their vital statistics - they are listed in order of increasing scores against the British Cycling (BC) Index of route intensity - explained later in this section.

Route		Km	Elev. (m)	m/km	BC Index	Miles	Feet	Terrain
1.	Lyme Park and the Middlewood Way	36.1	506	14.0	18.3	22.4	1660	5
2.	A Pinch of Salt	51.6	364	7.1	18.8	32.1	1194	5
3.	Chelford Quarry and Marton Bridleways	48.2	439	9.1	21.2	30.0	1440	5
4.	Delamere Forest Delight	49.8	435	8.7	21.7	30.9	1427	6
5.	Laureen's Ride	60.9	418	6.9	25.5	37.8	1371	6
6.	Mersey Paradise	64.7	458	7.1	29.6	40.2	1503	5
7.	Biddulph Valley Way, Rudyard and Bosley Cloud	50.6	631	12.5	31.9	31.4	2070	7
8.	Cown Edge and The Peak Forest Canal	43.5	806	18.5	35.1	27.0	2644	6
9.	Chewing Gravel	39.3	976	24.8	38.4	24.4	3202	7
10.	Nantwich Canal-fest	74.4	519	7.0	38.6	46.2	1703	5
11.	Tatton Park and the TPT to Runcorn	84.2	636	7.6	53.6	52.3	2087	5
12.	Macc Forest Monster	49.3	1302	26.4	64.2	30.6	4272	7
13.	Chester, Canals and Chemicals	87.4	742	8.5	64.9	54.3	2434	5

Climb and Route Intensity Metrics

I use three different metrics to describe the difficulty of each of the routes and their constituent climbs.

1) British Cycling (BC) Index

This measure is typically used for grading the difficulty of sportive events; it is simply the distance of the ride (in km) multiplied by the total elevation gain (in km), as illustrated in the table below - the relative positions of the above routes are overlaid on the table.

2) Climbing Intensity of the Route

The metric for climbing intensity is the of total metres of elevation gain divided by the total distance of the ride in kilometres - with guideline values as follows:

Metric	Description	Colour-code
Less than 10m/km	A fairly flat ride	Blue
Between 10m/km and 20m/km	Signifies a moderately hilly ride	Amber
Between 20m/km and 25m/km	Signifies a ride with a lot of climbing	Red
Over 25m/km	A very intense ride (typically full of Black climbs - see below)	Black

3) Hill Grading Method

The method used to grade the notable climbs for the routes is from www.climbbybike.com, whereby:

$$\text{CBB INDEX} = 2\times (H\times100/D) + H^2/D + D/1000$$

H = elevation gain (m); D = distance (m)

Therefore, short and shallow hills score low; steep and long hills score high; long but no-so-steep hills (or steep but short hills) score somewhere in the middle.

Using the above index method and applying to the local hills, the climb colour-grading is:

Metric	Colour-code
Index score greater than 5, but less than 15	Blue
Index score greater than 15, but less than 30	Red
Index score greater than 30	Black

Here is an example of how this works in practice:

- A climb ascending 200m over 2km scores 42, therefore Black
- A climb ascending 200m over 4km scores 24, therefore Red
- A climb ascending 100m over 2km scores 17, therefore also Red
- A climb ascending 100m over 4km scores 11.5, therefore Blue

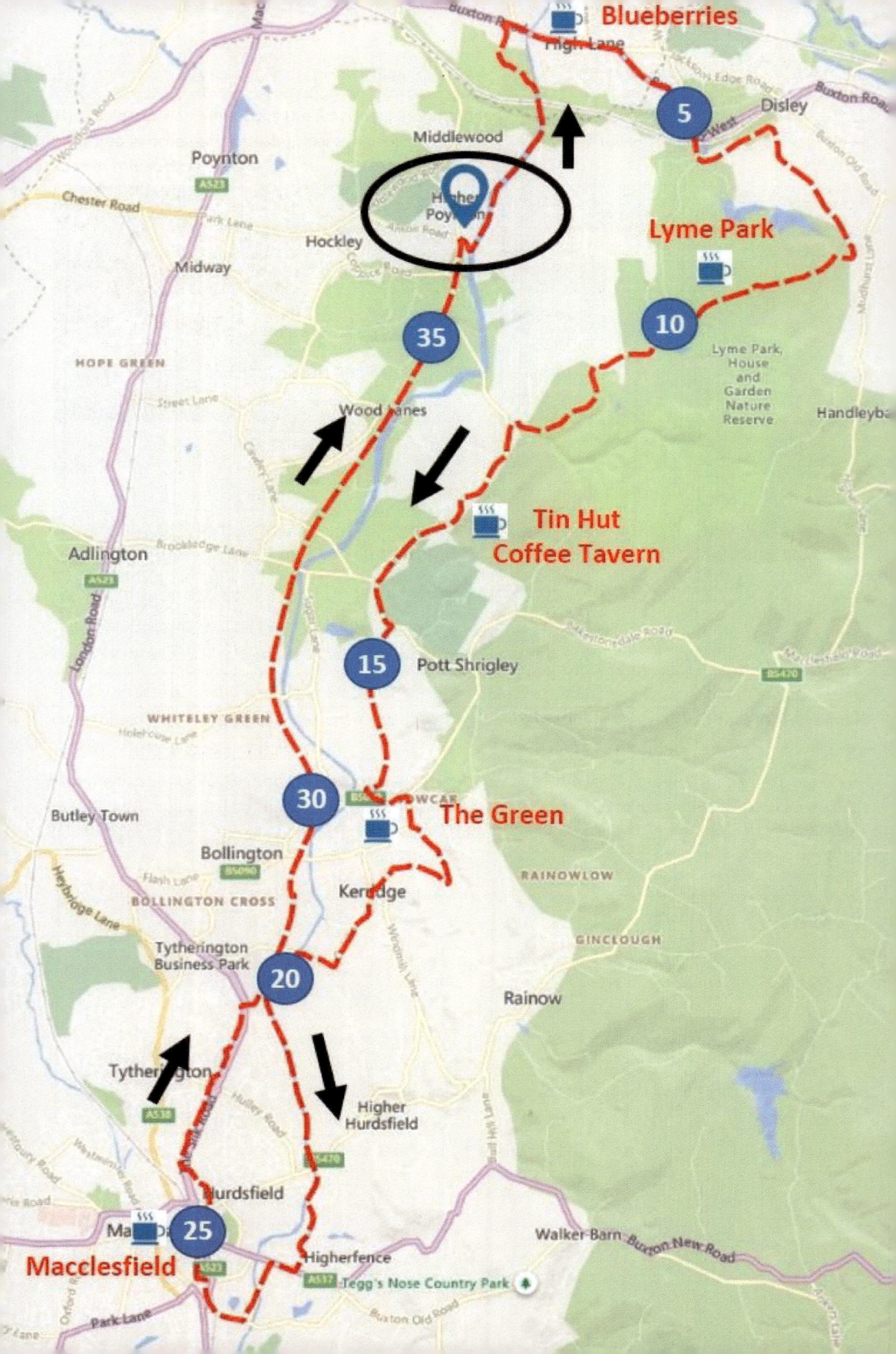

Blueberries

5

Disley

Lyme Park

10

Lyme Park, House and Garden Nature Reserve

35

Wood Lanes

Tin Hut Coffee Tavern

15

Pott Shrigley

30

Bollington

The Green

Kerridge

20

Tytherington Business Park

Higher Hurdsfield

Hurdsfield

25

Macclesfield

Higherfence

Tegg's Nose Country Park

1) LYME PARK AND THE MIDDLEWOOD WAY

Dist. (km)	Elev. (m)	m/km	BC Index	Miles	Feet	Terrain
36.1	506	14.0	18.3	22.4	1660	5

Route Start-point: Nelson Pit Visitor Centre, Higher Poynton

Alternative Start-points: Lyme Park, Bollington, Macclesfield

Ideal Bike: Great on either a Gravel Bike or MTB (majority of off-road sections drain well)

Stop-off Options: Blueberries (High Lane), Lyme Park, Tin Hut Coffee Tavern (Pott Shrigley), The Green (Bollington), Macclesfield (lots)

This route offers a mix of four notable climbs together with long sections of flat riding, including the Macclesfield Canal towpath and the Middlewood Way.

The highlights of the route include: a tour through Lyme Park, an off-road climb around White Nancy and 10km along The Middlewood Way from Macclesfield to Higher Poynton.

Note: Please check the opening/closing times for Lyme Park before embarking on this route.

The Low-down on the Climbs

The elevation profile for the route is illustrated in the diagram below, highlighting the key climbs.

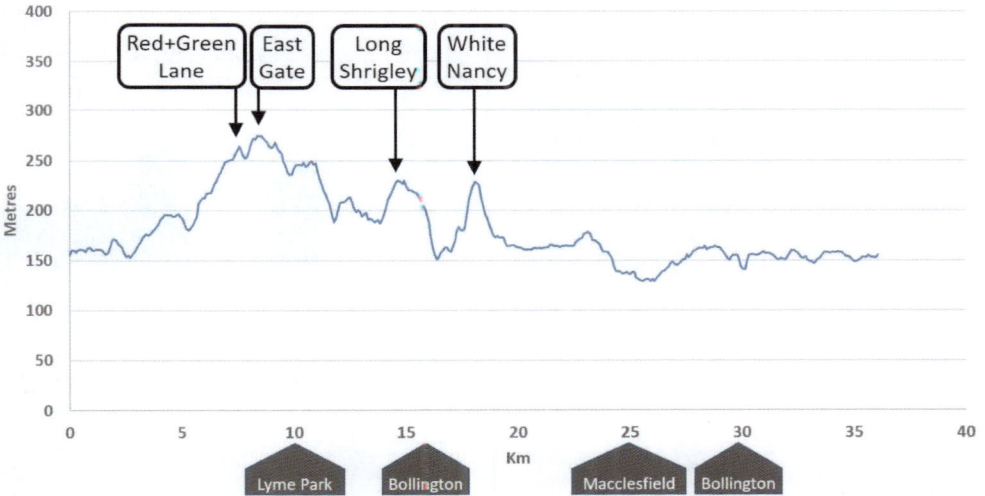

There are four notable climbs, including one Black, on this route, their vital statistics are listed below.

Climb	Distance (m)	Elevation Gain (m)	Peak Gradient	CBB Index	Features
Red + Green Lane	2200	82	7%	12.7	Steady gravel climb, narrow in places with a few larger stones to dodge
East Gate	600	32	12%	13.0	Single-track gravel climb
Long Shrigley	700	47	11%	17.3	Steady road climb
White Nancy	400	58	20%	37.8	Short but very steep tarmacked climb with (slippery) cattle grids to negotiate

Places of Interest on the Route

Middlewood Way

This is a trail reclaimed from the former Macclesfield, Bollington and Marple Railway, it runs for 16km between Marple and Macclesfield and has a surface mix of tarmac and hard-packed gravel.

Lyme Park

Lyme Park is a 1400-acre estate owned by the National Trust. It dates from the 14th century and has an impressive mansion house. The grounds are also home to a large herd of deer - often seen on a bike ride!

White Nancy

A distinctive landmark on top of Kerridge Hill, built in 1817 to commemorate the Battle of Waterloo.

Route Narrative

This route starts from the Nelson Pit Visitor Centre in Higher Poynton - there is a large carpark, or you can park in the layby opposite the Boar's Head at quieter times.

For almost 2km, the route follows the canal towpath heading north before bearing off to the left along a double-track gravel lane to meet the A6 in High Lane. The route then has a steady climb for 2km along the A6 to reach the main entrance to Lyme Park, it then descends the driveway to reach the gate that leads onto the first climb. The climb up Red Lane is tarmacked and steady in gradient.

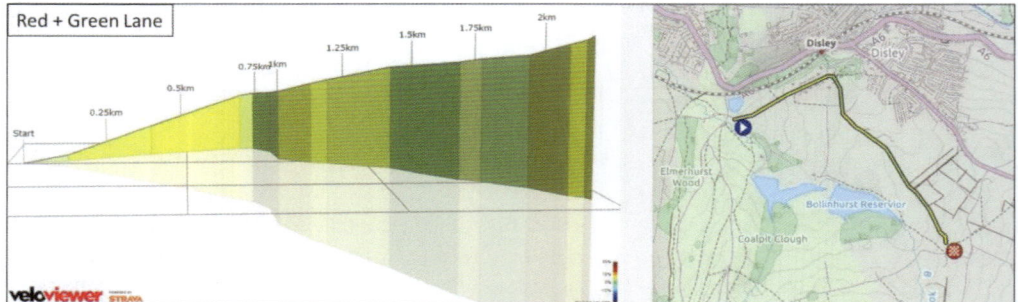

After turning the corner onto Green Lane, the surface turns to gravel initially and then becomes a single-track path (photo below) to reach a gate, after which the path widens for the last part of the trail (note that this part used to be rutted and rocky but was levelled and filled in early 2020).

There is another gate at the end that leads onto another track that heads east to reach the East Gate entrance to Lyme Park (this is another track that was rocky but was levelled and filled in early 2020). Before reaching the East Gate, the trail descends to a bridge (dismount required to cross) and then climbs back up to reach the East Gate.

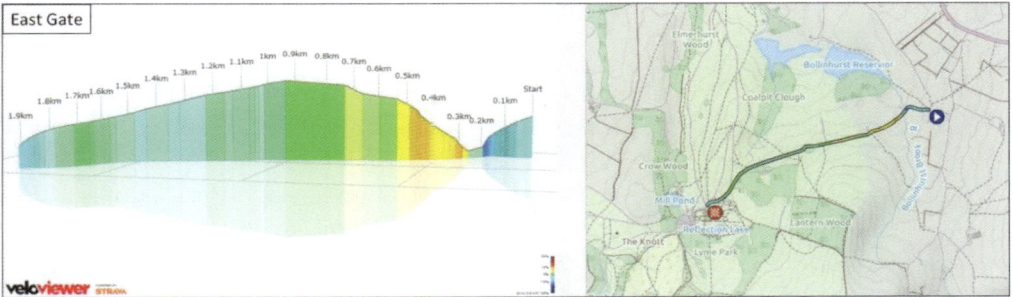

You then pass through the East Gate to enter Lyme Park (check opening times) and continue along a gravel track that becomes tarmacked and offers fantastic views (photo below).

When you reach Lyme Hall, follow the road around to the right, take a left to descend past the carpark (take a detour to the café if you wish to stop) and then climb up the other side in a westerly direction along Old West Park Drive for 0.5km. The route then goes through the wooden gate by the small carpark and treats you to a fabulous descent on a wide gravel track all the way down to the park's West Gate.

The route now joins the road for a short climb over the top of Shrigley Road before descending and proceeding along the flat for a further kilometre. Just as you approach the next junction, the road rises up again for the next instalment of climbing on a segment named "Long Shrigley", which continues up Shrigley Road alongside Pott Shrigley Golf Club and then turns right onto Long Lane to climb up the side of Nab Head.

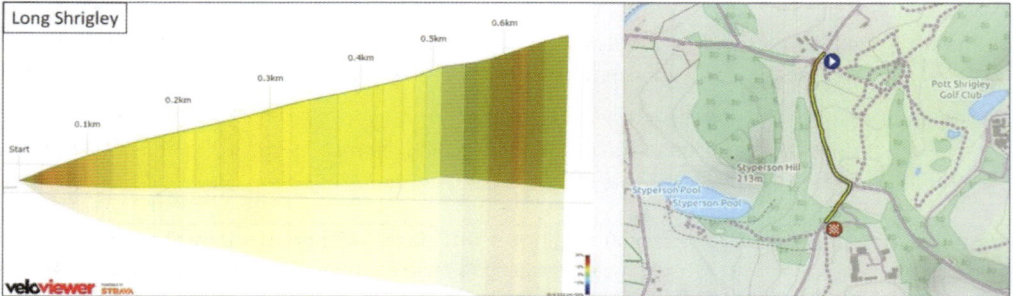

Once over the top, the lane descends - getting steeper as you progress - with a surprise in store around after the right-hand corner… The road surface becomes cobbled just before a sharp hairpin bend - so be prepared, scrub-off the necessary speed and pick your line carefully!

At the bottom of the hill, you take a left turn onto Palmerston Street to climb through the centre of Bollington - with several cafes if you wish to stop. A right turn at the roundabout leads onto Church Street that leads to Ingersley Vale, which has a gravel surface and takes you to the start of the toughest climb of the ride - around White Nancy.

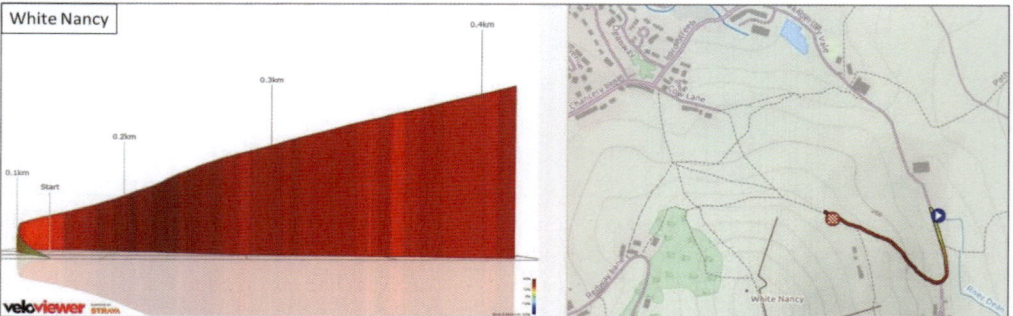

After rounding the initial corner of this climb, the gradient ramps up dramatically to around 20% - dig deep and keep climbing - the views from the top are worth it (photo below)!

The track then emerges onto the hairpin bend of Redway Lane, where you take a series of left turns to reach the towpath of the Macclesfield Canal, which involves a spiral ramp descent (photo below).

After 2.5km, the route leaves the canal (by steps) to join Higher Fence Road for a bit more gravel and a road-tour around residential southern Macclesfield to reach Sunderland Street.

You now join the Middlewood Way section of Route 55 in Macclesfield town centre for a convoluted (but traffic-free) route out of the town. The initial section is tarmacked as you skirt around Tytherington and cross The Silk Road via the bridge and zig-zag ramps. The surface then changes to gravel as you head towards and through Bollington. As you ride through Bollington, the Middlewood Way crosses the old railway viaduct - which offers great views (photo below).

It's plain sailing for the rest of the way, with no more hills or obstacles to overcome as you head north through Wood Lanes to reach Higher Poynton and return to the start.

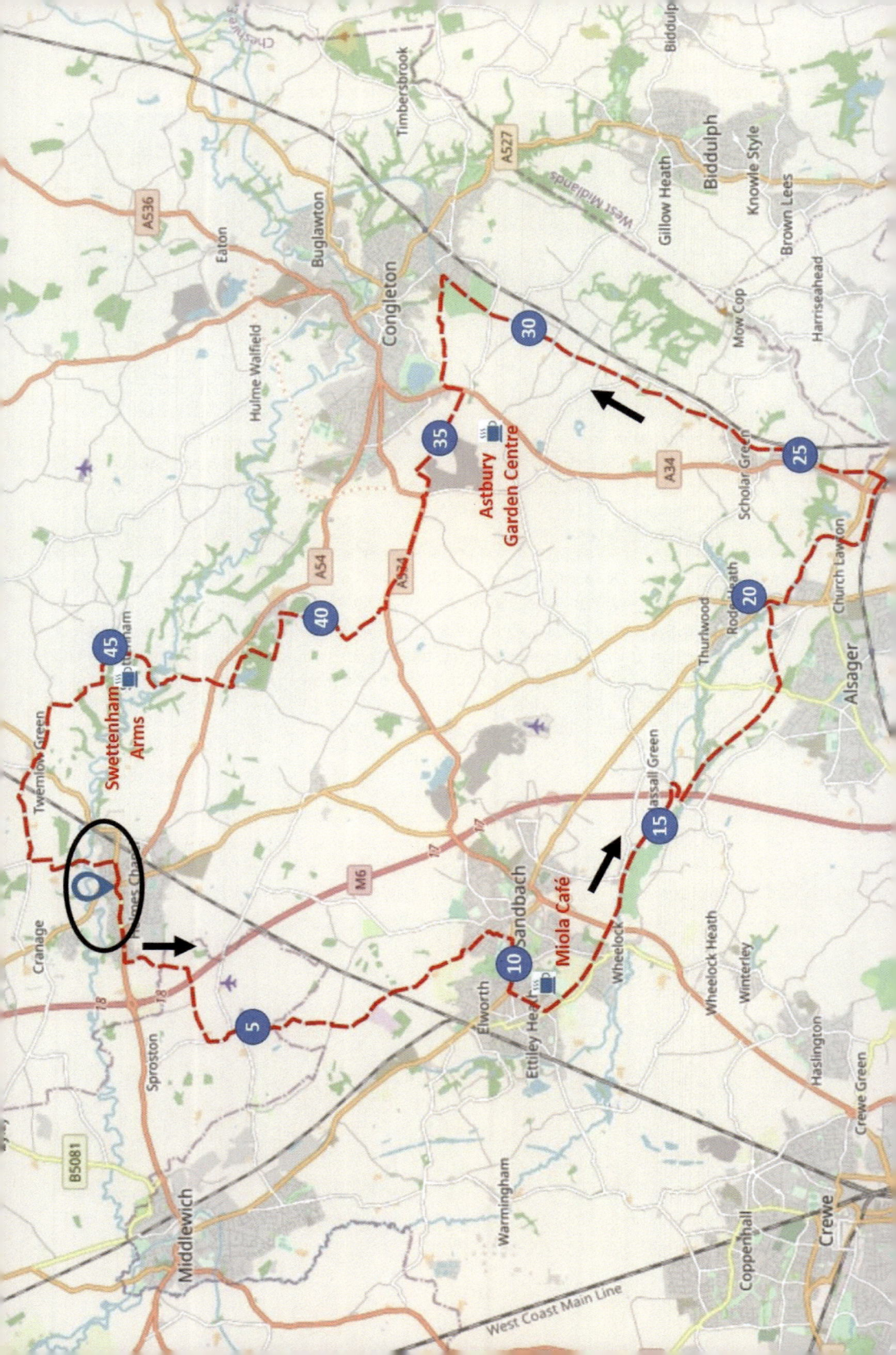

2) A PINCH OF SALT

Dist. (km)	Elev. (m)	m/km	BC Index	Miles	Feet	Terrain
51.6	364	7.1	18.8	32.1	1194	5

Route Start-point: Costa Coffee, Holmes Chapel

Alternative Start-points: Swettenham Arms, Brereton Heath, Astbury Garden Centre

Ideal Bike: Great on either a Gravel Bike or MTB (towpaths become muddy during wetter months)

Stop-off Options: Miola Café (Sandbach), Astbury Garden Centre, Swettenham Arms

This traces Cheshire's history of salt with a ride along the former railway line that used to serve the salt works at Malkin's Bank. It is a route without major climbs that strings together several off-road sections including the Wheelock Rail Trail, the Salt Line; towpaths on the Trent and Mersey and the Macclesfield Canals; several bridleways south west of Congleton; and a great trail through Davenport Park.

The Low-down on the Climbs

The elevation profile for the route is illustrated in the diagram below, there are no notable climbs.

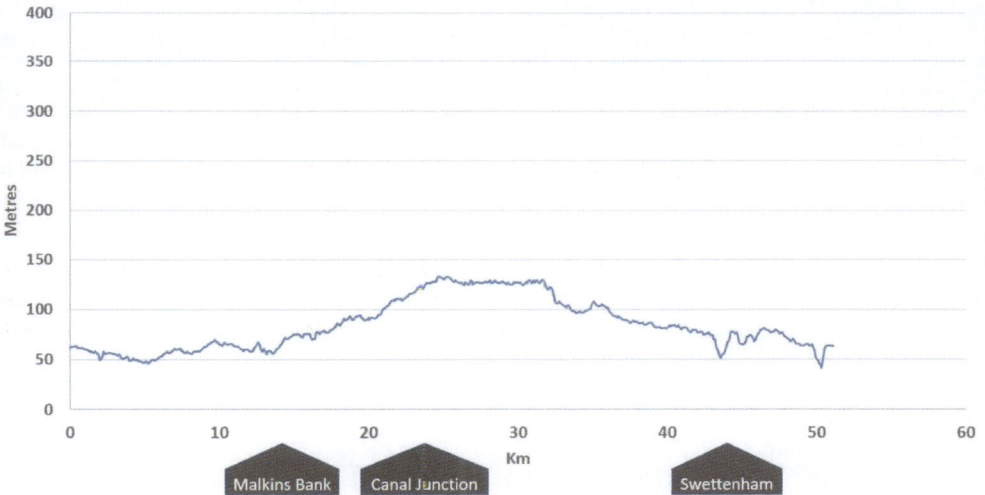

Places of Interest on the Route

Wheelock Rail Trail and The Salt Line
These are multi-user trails resurrected from the former North Staffordshire Railway branch line that ran in between Kidsgrove and Sandbach, serving the Malkin's Bank Salt Works, and was closed in 1966.

Trent and Mersey Canal
This canal was opened in 1777 and runs for 150km linking the River Trent in Derbyshire to the Bridgewater Canal at Preston Brook. It is managed by the Canal and River Trust, so cycling is permitted along the whole of its length. The canal also features a 2.6km tunnel near Kidsgrove and has a total of 76 locks.

Macclesfield Canal
This canal is more recent, opening in 1831 and connects the Trent & Mersey Canal (near Kidsgrove) with the Peak Forest Canal (in Marple). It runs for 42km and has a single flight of 12 locks by Bosley (that make for an exhilarating descent on a bike along the towpath - included in Route 3). It is also managed by the Canal and River Trust.

Route Narrative

This route starts from the double-roundabout junction in Holmes Chapel (by Costa Coffee - parking is available in London Road Car Park, a short distance south along the A50). You follow a series of lanes for the initial 11km as you head south towards Sandbach. The route then joins National Cycle Route 5 for the first off-road section - The Wheelock Rail Trail, which offers fast-rolling smooth tarmac - photo below. Note that there are 2 road junctions along this section that will require a dismount to cross.

The rail trail lasts for just over 2km before it links up with the Trent and Mersey Canal, temporarily departing from Route 5 for the next 2km as you follow the canal. The towpath is in reasonable condition but note that there are several locks - each with a steep section of cobbles to ascend.

The next off-road section is the Salt Line, which offers a further 2km of smooth-rolling path. Cherry Lane then continues to follow Route 5, which leads to the towpath along The Trent and Mersey Canal. The route follows the southern side of the canal for a kilometre before crossing over a bridge to the other side of the canal. The towpath is gravel-based and reasonably smooth-rolling (photo below).

After a further 2.5km, you reach the junction between the Trent and Mersey Canal and the Macclesfield Canal, which involves a complicated series of spiral bridge crossings that takes you onto the western side of the Macclesfield Canal heading in a northerly direction.

This next section of canal lasts for 8km. This is a rural stretch of the route with great scenery, the surface along the towpath is variable along the way and can be bumpy (muddy if wet) in places (photo below).

There are also several bridges to negotiate along the towpath that require care and concentration - the bridges are low in height and typically offer a choice of a cobbled surface away from the water or uneven flag-stones next to the water (photo below).

As you approach Congleton, the route leaves the canal via a flight of steps (dismount required) to join Lamberts Lane. This offers an exhilarating single-track descent for 1.5km (photo below), but please be mindful of walkers and horse-riders along this track.

At the end of the track, you join a short section of road that leads to the A34, which then leads to a right turn onto Bent Lane. This lane leads to a farm and then onto a gravel track, which then takes a left turn through a gate onto a tree-lined single-track path that leads to Walhill Lane and its junction with the A534.

You then follow the main road for 2km and then turn right onto Smethwick Lane, which leads onto Moss Lane and in turn onto Brereton Heath Lane. The route then picks up a bridleway that leads into Brereton Heath - in dry conditions this is fast flowing and fabulous; in wet conditions this can become really boggy (and great practice if you want to test your bike handling skills!). If the ground is really wet, then skip this bridleway by continuing to the end of the lane and turning right onto Davenport Lane.

You then join Regional Cycle Route 71 and cross the A54 to enter the spectacular Davenport Park (photo).

The route follows the driveway and bears right down a single-track path alongside a series of ponds to reach a bridge over the River Dane. You then climb up the other side, initially on a gravel path and then along a tarmacked lane to reach the village of Swettenham (with an optional stop at the Swettenham Arms). After the village, you turn left onto a gravel lane that leads to a right turn onto a single-track path with a short, steep climb (photo below) that joins Cross Lane for a rural return towards Twemlow Green.

The final section of the route follows another gravel-based double-track lane back down over the River Dane and up the other side to return into Holmes Chapel.

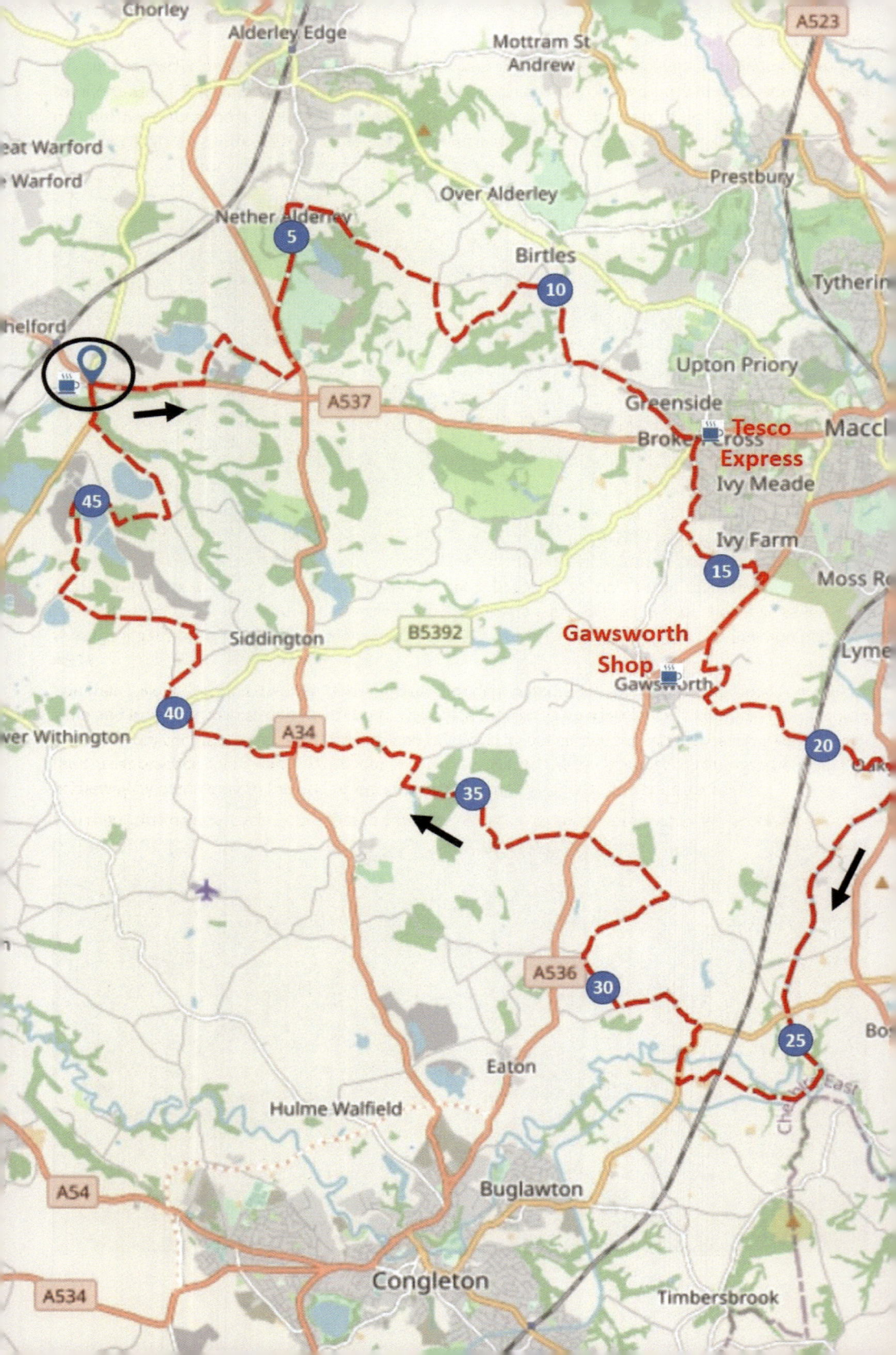

3) CHELFORD QUARRY AND THE BOSLEY LOCKS

Dist. (km)	Elev. (m)	m/km	BC Index	_Miles_	_Feet_	_Terrain_
48.2	439	9.1	21.2	30.0	1440	5

Route Start-point: Chelford Corner Shoppe (A537 / A535 junction)

Alternative Start-points: Nether Alderley, Broken Cross, Gawsworth, Marton

Ideal Bike: Great on either a Gravel Bike or MTB (becomes very muddy after wet weather)

Stop-off Options: Tesco Express (Broken Cross), Gawsworth Shop

This is a fairly flat route with two Blue climbs that mixes-in a great range of off-road sections and offers some surprising local scenery. **Note that several sections can become very muddy after wet weather.**

The Low-down on the Climbs

The elevation profile for the route is illustrated in the diagram below, highlighting the key climbs.

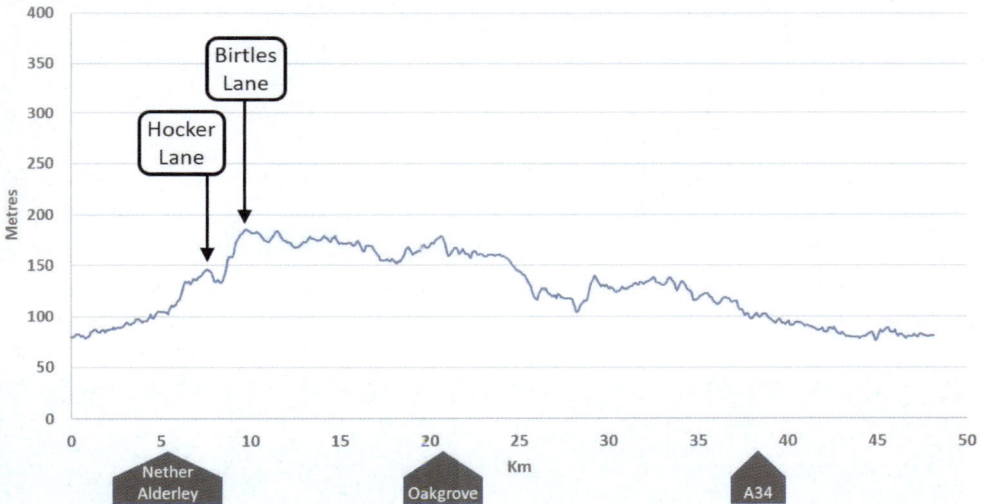

There are two notable climbs on this route, their vital statistics are listed below.

Climb	Distance (m)	Elevation Gain (m)	Peak Gradient	CBB Index	Features
Hocker Lane	2000	41	7%	6.9	Steady climb with a mix of cobbles and hard-packed gravel
Birtles Lane	1000	50	8%	13.5	Steady road climb

Places of Interest on the Route

Alderley Park

The former AstraZeneca research site, covering 350 acres, is now a multi-tenanted site with a mix of business, residential and leisure facilities. The woods off Hocker Lane are now open for public use and include an array of paths permissible for cycling.

Henbury Hall

This hall was built in the 1980's, replacing the original 18th century hall, under the ownership of the Ferranti family. A previous owner (Thomas Brocklehurst) reputedly imported a pair of grey squirrels in 1876 - to the (almost) seal the fate of the red squirrel!

Bosley Locks

This is a flight of 12 locks along the Macclesfield Canal, within a 4km stretch with a combined elevation change of 36m. The locks have been in operation since 1831 make for an exhilarating descent on a bike!

Chelford Quarry

This quarry has yielded 60 million tonnes of sand over its 60 years of production, it has now ceased operation and will be restored to a natural environment - hopefully with public access and a range of new bridleways...

Route Narrative

The route follows the A537 for the initial 1.4km and then turns left onto Stubby Lane for the first section of off-road riding, which is mainly double-track - it is prone to puddles when wet, some of which can be deep after persistent rain. At the end of this section, you turn right onto the tarmacked Bollington Lane.

You then join the A34 and then take the second exit at the roundabout to follow the old main road towards Alderley Edge, passing by Alderley Park and the 16th century Nether Alderley Mill. A right turn then takes you onto Bradford Lane for the next off-road section and the first climb of the route.

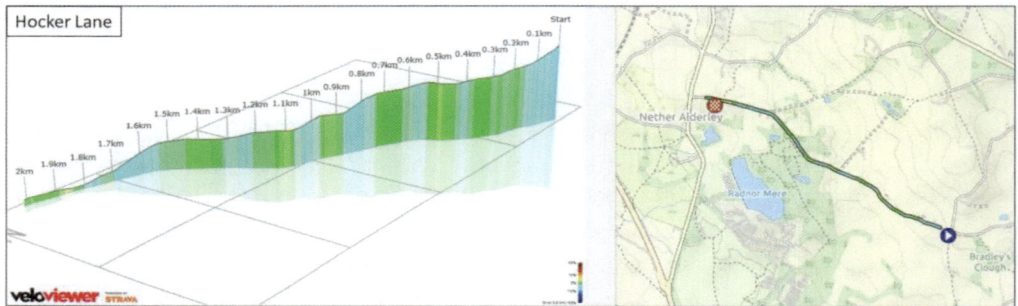

The section along Bradford Lane is cobbled and gradually increases in gradient as the lane progresses. When you reach the triangle junction, bear right onto Hocker Lane, where the surface changes to hard-packed gravel (photo below).

The climb continues for 2km at a gentle gradient and finishes with a rougher cobbled section, after which the route turns right down a muddy double-track lane (it can get really muddy in the winter) to reach a gate by a farm. After the gate, the track has a firmer gravel surface and descends gently to meet Birtles Lane, where you turn left and encounter the second climb of the route up Birtles Lane.

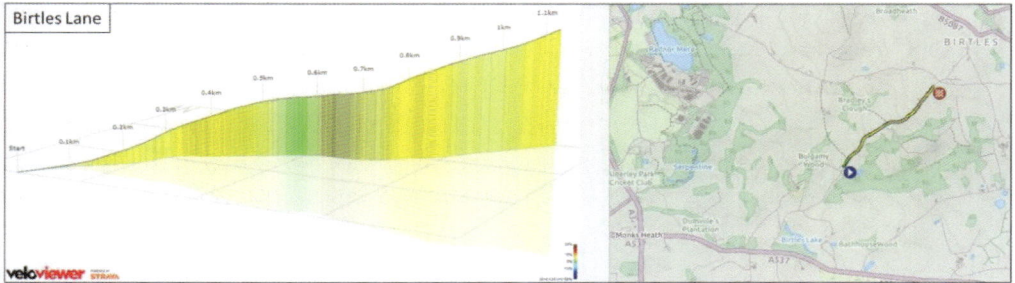

At the top of the climb, you turn right onto Cross Lane, which can become quite muddy, and then turn right again at the end to descend Wrigley Lane and Whirley Lane to reach Broken Cross.

From Broken Cross, the route heads in a southerly direction and follows Gawsworth Road for just over a kilometre. A left turn onto Penningtons Lane offers the next instalment of gravel.

The route now heads towards Gawsworth, initially along the A536 and then by taking a right-turn onto Lowes Lane, which bypasses the centre of the village and leads onto Woodhouse End Road heading east. Towards the end of this section, the road descends steeply around an S-bend and reaches a swing-bridge over the Macclesfield Canal - just prior to its junction with the A523. The route joins the canal prior to crossing the swing-bridge and heads in a southerly direction for 5km.

The highlight of this canal section is the flight of locks, which provides an exhilarating descent along the towpath. Note that the short slopes by each lock are fairly steep and comprise a range of surfaces including loose gravel and cobbles - these can be ridden very fast if you so choose, but can also present quite a challenge depending on the type of bike you are riding and your skill/appetite for sketchy terrain.

After the final lock, the landscape opens to present a great view to the south east, which is followed by a spectacular aqueduct that crosses high above the River Dane.

The route then leaves the towpath and follows a twisting single-track bridleway in a westerly direction that passes under the impressive viaduct (photo below) that carries the West Coast Mainline. You then pass through a farm and join the A54 for a kilometre before following a series of lanes for nearly 5km to reach the A536.

The next off-road section is just on the other side of the A536 and follows a double-track lane to a farm and then through some superb countryside (photo below).

The bridleway exits onto School Lane by the Marton Heath Trout Pools; you then turn right and then take a left turn after 400m onto the next gravel section, which follows another double-track gravel lane through another farm and more great countryside to reach the A34.

A right-and-first-left then leads away from the main road along Blackden Lane; you cross over Salters Lane onto Chapel Lane and then onto Moss Lane, which leads to a short bridleway (muddy when wet). At the end, you turn left onto the lane and head west for a mile. Just prior to the sharp bend, the route takes a right turn onto a bridleway that leads across a field (photo below - also muddy when wet).

The path across the field leads to the perimeter of Chelford Quarry. The route follows a single-track path around the quarry (very muddy when wet!), which offers fantastic views - it's one of those places that you'd never know was there!

The path then emerges onto the northern side of Lapwing Lane, turns right and then takes a left onto another (potentially muddy) bridleway that leads through a wooded area to reach Congleton Lane. A left turn then takes you back to join the A535 for a short distance to return to the start.

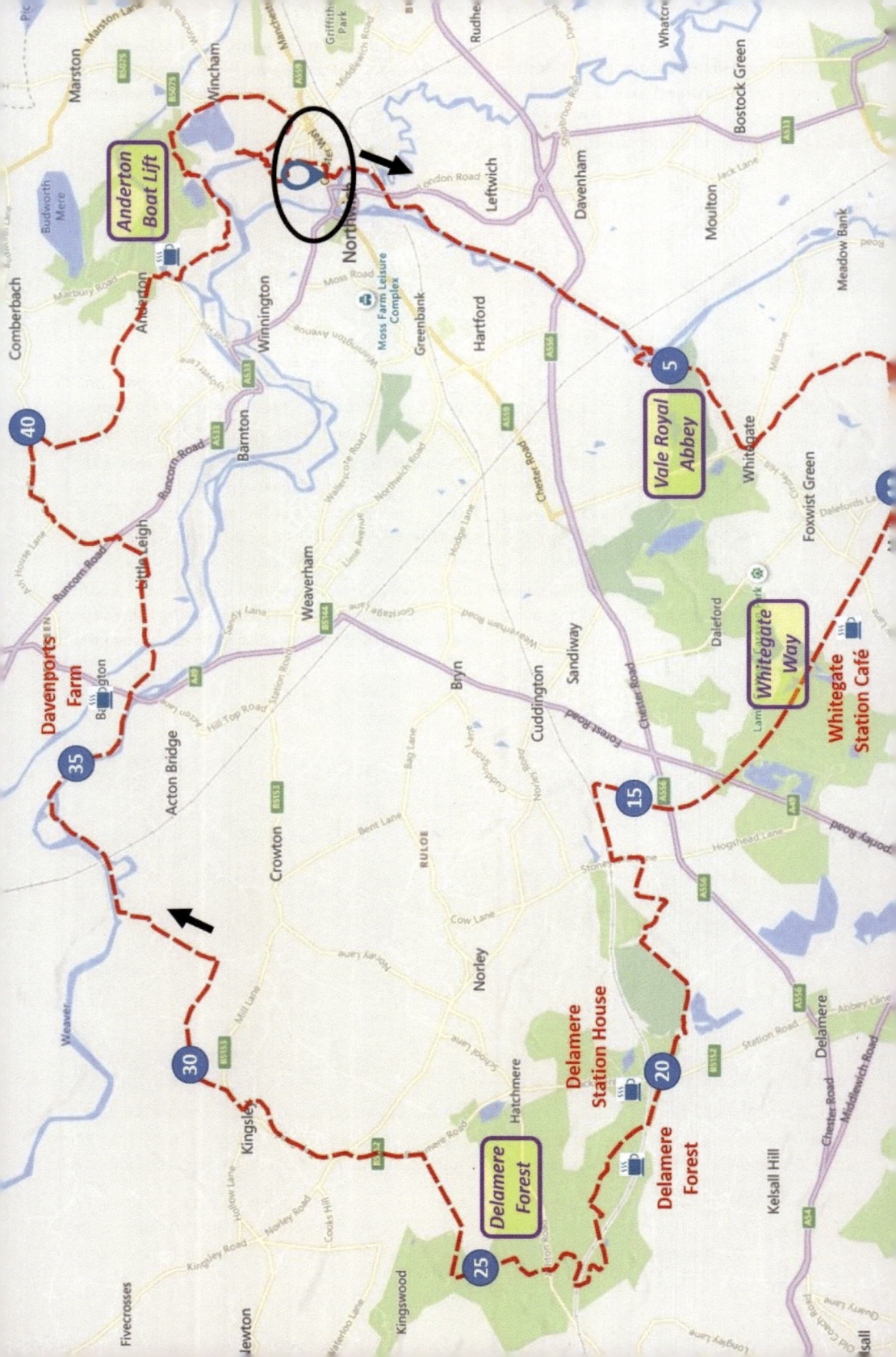

Anderton Boat Lift

Vale Royal Abbey

Whitegate Way

Whitegate Station Café

Davenports Farm

Delamere Station House

Delamere Forest

Delamere Forest

5

15

20

25

30

35

40

Marston
Wincham
Comberbach
Budworth Mere
Marbury Road
Anderton
Winnington
Barnton
Little Leigh
Runcorn Road
Barnton
Acton Bridge
Bartington
Crowton
Kingsley
Weaver
Newton
Fivecrosses
Kingswood
Northwich
Hartford
Greenbank
Moss Farm Leisure Complex
Weaverham
Bryn
Cuddington
Sandiway
Norley
Hatchmere
Ruloe
Cow Lane
London Road
Leftwich
Davenham
Moulton
Meadow Bank
Whitegate
Foxwist Green
Daleford
Dalefords Lane
Hogshead Lane
Delamere
Kelsall Hill
Rudheath
Whatcroft
Bostock Green
Jack Lane
Chester Road
Forest Road
Station Road

4) DELAMERE FOREST DELIGHT

Dist. (km)	Elev. (m)	m/km	BC Index	Miles	Feet	Terrain
49.8	435	8.7	21.7	30.9	1427	6

Route Start-point: Northwich Memorial Car Park

Alternative Start-points: Whitegate Station, Delamere Forest, Anderton Boat Lift

Stop-off Options: Whitegate Station Café, Delamere Forest, Davenports Farm, Anderton Boat Lift

Ideal Bike: Gravel bike (MTB also ok - preferred after wet weather)

This route offers a great mix of off-road riding, such as the path along the River Weaver, the fabulous Whitegate Way, the amazing Oakmere Way, the stunning Delamere Forest and the great section of trail around Dutton Locks (as you might be able to tell... this is one of my favourite routes!)

The Low-down on the Climbs

The elevation profile for the route is illustrated in the diagram below, there is one notable climb.

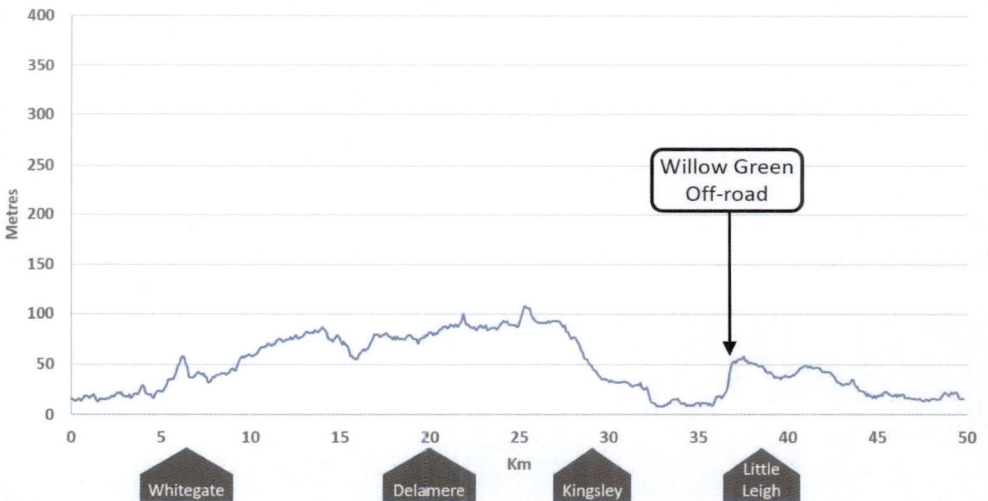

Climb	Distance (m)	Elevation Gain (m)	Peak Gradient	CBB Index	Features
Willow Green Off-road	600	37	12%	15.2	Fairly steep and narrow gravel climb, gets muddy when wet

Places of Interest on the Route

Delamere Forest

The largest area of woodland in England at 972 hectares (2,400 acres); Delamere Forest is now a fraction of its former size - it once covered 160km² (60 square miles)! The use of the forest dates from Anglo-Saxon times and it has been used extensively for hunting purposes such as for wild boar and deer.

Nowadays, it is a popular leisure location offering a range of trails for walkers, runners, horse-riding and off-road cycling. The forest also contains The Old Pale hill, which is the highest point of the northern section of the Mid Cheshire Ridge and is used as a music venue.

There is also a modern visitor centre just south of the route that has cycle hire and equipment, as well as a café, picnic area and toilets.

Anderton Boat Lift

Known as the "Cathedral of the Canals", the boat lift was originally built in 1875 to provide a 15m (50') vertical waterway connection between the River Weaver and the Trent and Mersey Canal. After serving over 100 years, the lift was restored and reopened in 2002 along with a visitor centre and exhibition.

Vale Royal Abbey

This is a county house with a history that dates back to 1270 as a medieval abbey that was originally destined to be a similar scale to Westminster Abbey by King Edward I, but a series of wars, political change and natural disasters thwarted the plans. It is now a popular wedding venue in the grounds of Vale Royal Golf Club.

Whitegate Way

This is a 10km bridleway that traces the route of the Winsford and Over Branch Line that operated from 1870 until 1967, serving passengers and the numerous salt works around Winsford. Whitegate station now houses a visitor centre and a café - it also has a carpark.

Route Narrative

From the carpark in Northwich, the route initially follows an off-road cycleway through a park and then to the side of the railway to join National Cycle Route 5 as it follows the River Weaver upstream.

The route continues to follow the river for the next 3.5km to reach Vale Royal Locks, where you cross over the locks and then climb up Vale Royal Drive to ride past the stunning Vale Royal Abbey.

Vale Royal Drive then continues to the left of the road in the form of a short section of double-track through the trees, follow this down and emerge onto Whitegate Lane before taking a left turn almost immediately onto Grange Lane. This lane starts tarmacked and then becomes a single-track bridleway that offers a fantastic adventure through the woods and then links up with the Whitegate Way.

The scenery along the Whitegate Way gets better and better as you progress along it (see photo) - enjoy!

After around 7km, you approach the end of the Whitegate Way and take a left turn down a flight of wooden steps to join the Oakmere Way, which offers an amazing single-track experience (photo) for 4.5km with great views over the Cheshire Sands Quarry and across to Delamere Forest.

The Oakmere Way exits onto the B5152 opposite the driveway that leads to the main entrance to Delamere Forest. The following 5km follows a series of cycle paths through the forest, along hard-packed gravel paths surrounded by great scenery without any major climbs.

The route then exits the northern side of the forest onto Hondslough Lane, which leads onto a series of lanes through Kingsley and onwards to Pickering's Lock to join a gravel track along the River Weaver (photo below).

The route follows the track on the southern side of the river for 1.3km, which has a gravel surface and is prone to puddles after wet weather. You then cross over the river at Dutton Locks, after which the surface is tarmacked and continues for almost 2km before reaching the A49 by the Acton Swing Bridge.

Take care crossing the road (frequently busy with fast-moving traffic) and proceed in an easterly direction onto Willow Green Lane, leading back out into the countryside.

This lane starts along the flat and then starts to ramp up as you approach the bridge over the Trent & Mersey Canal for the start of the only notable climb on this route.

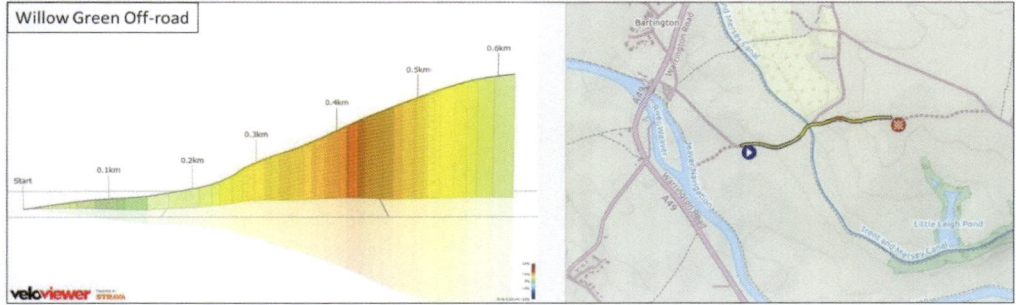

The gradient of the climb increases as you cross over the canal, you then take a right turn onto a bridleway that steepens and presents a reasonable challenge on a gravel bike - particularly so after wet weather as the steep section can become muddy. After you emerge at the top of the climb, the track widens and becomes a double-track gravel lane that leads onto Leigh Lane (on the Cheshire Cycleway) heading into Little Leigh.

You then cross the A533 and follow a series of lanes to reach the driveway that leads to the Anderton Boat Lift (there is a café at the boat lift if you wish to stop). You then follow a marvellous series of gravel tracks around Northwich Community Woodlands (photo below) - 373 hectares of accessible countryside.

The route does a complete loop around Neumann's Flash and Ashton's Flash, that were once used by ICI to store lime waste but have now been returned to nature and support a wide diversity of wildlife. You then exit the woodlands onto Leicester Street and then Venables Road to join Chester Way and return to the start.

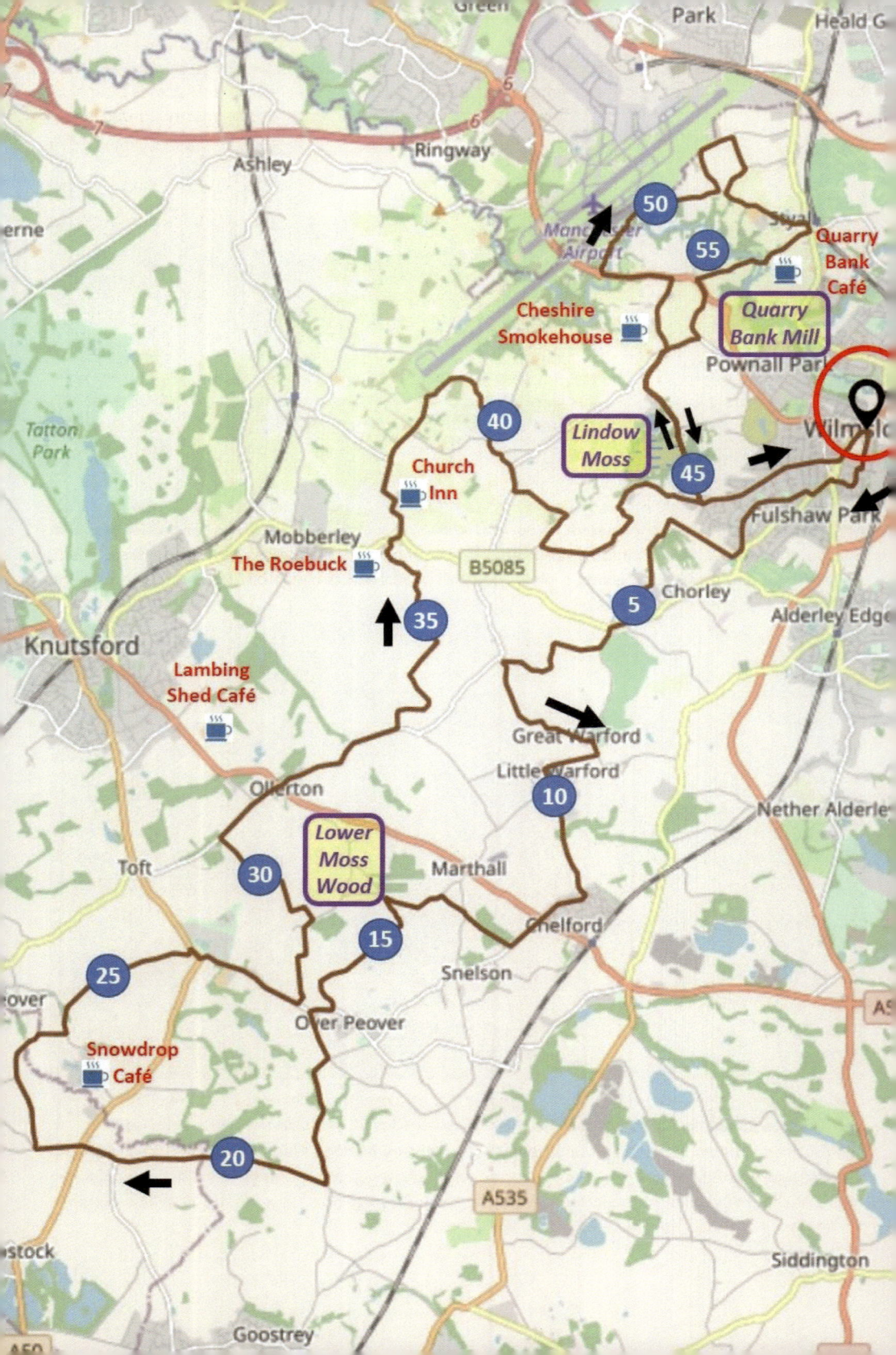

5) LAUREEN'S RIDE

Dist. (km)	Elev. (m)	m/km	BC Index	Miles	Feet	Terrain
60.9	418	6.9	25.5	37.8	1371	6

Route Start-point: Costa Coffee (Wilmslow Town Centre)

Alternative Start-points: Warford, Mobberley, Quarry Bank Mill (Styal)

Ideal Bike: Gravel bike after dry weather, MTB when wet

Stop-off Options: Snowdrop Café (Grasslands Garden Centre), Lambing Shed Café (Knutsford), Roebuck (Mobberley), Church Inn (Mobberley), Cheshire Smokehouse (Morley Green), Quarry Bank Café.

Laureen's Ride is named after Laureen Roberts, who designed the ride whilst off work with a broken leg in 2011 and won the support for the route to be signposted and named after her. It is primarily a long-distance horse-riding route, but also makes a great route for riding on a gravel/hybrid/mountain bike!

There are two waymarked routes that intersect for a short distance; this route combines both into a single ride – with a slight extension to start and finish in Wilmslow town centre.

Note that several sections of the route become very muddy during the winter months.

The Low-down on the Climbs

The elevation profile for the route is illustrated in the diagram below, highlighting the one notable climb.

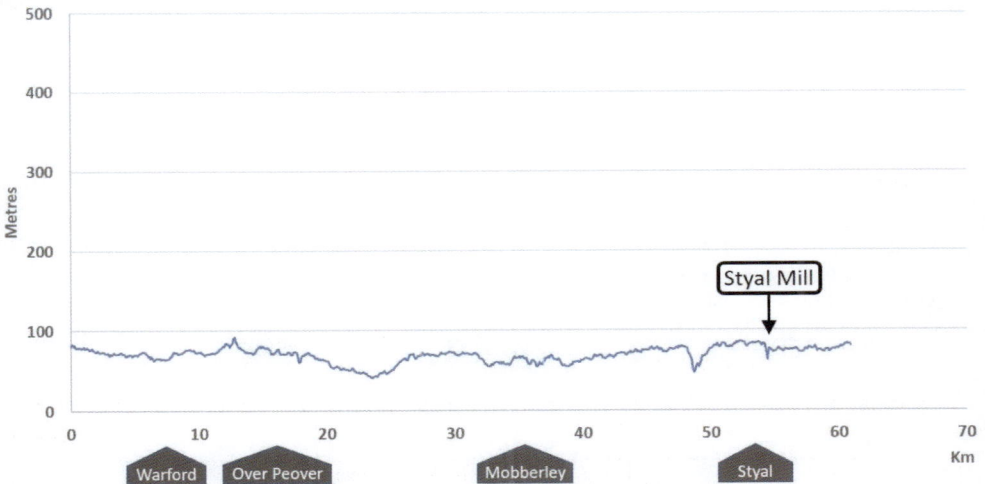

Climb	Dist. (m)	Elev. (m)	Peak Gradient	CBB Index	Notes
Styal Mill towards Honey Bee	200	22	19%	24.6	Short but very steep with steps

Places of Interest on the Route

Lower Moss Wood

This is an 18-acre nature reserve that also has an education facility (used by local schools and scout groups) and a wildlife hospital that treats around 2000 animal and bird casualties each year. It is also one of the most important sites for dragonflies in Cheshire.

Lindow Moss

This is a peat bog that is best known for the discovery of Lindow Man (also named "Pete Marsh") in 1984, who was brutally killed around 2,000 years ago and is the most well-preserved "bog body" discovered in the UK (complete with facial hair, manicured fingernails, healthy teeth and stomach contents).

Quarry Bank Mill, Styal

Built in 1784 as a factory to spin cotton, the mill is now owned by the National Trust and open to visitors throughout the year. In addition to the mill building, there is also an Apprentice House that tells the story of the lives of children working in the mill. The mill was also the inspiration for the 2013 TV drama "The Mill". There is also a gift shop and a café.

Route Narrative

This ride starts from Costa Coffee in the centre of Wilmslow and heads south west out of the town via

Holly Road South, Knutsford Road and Gravel Lane. As you approach the Horse and Jockey pub near the end of Gravel Lane, take a right turn (watch out for oncoming traffic around the bend) onto a gravel path after the pub and cut through to join Upcast Lane towards Lindow Cricket Club – you are now on the Heritage Loop of Laureen's Ride, so watch out for the purple signs!

Immediately opposite the cricket club, turn right onto a bridle path that leads out into the countryside, then turn left at the T-junction at the end onto a wider gravel track. Follow the track along around an S-bend and then bear left onto a narrow track into the trees (photo below). At the end of the path, the route joins Edge View Lane, which leads along to a junction with Knutsford Road.

The route stays on the road for the next 4.5km, which includes the intriguingly-named "Noah's Ark Lane". The route leaves Laureen's Heritage Loop at the junction with Ancoats Lane to join the Cheshire Cheese Loop on the way to that route's official start point at the end of Mill Lane.

Just after passing the David Lewis Centre, the route turns left onto a gated track and then turns right after 500m through a small gate into a field. Proceed across the field and down to cross a bridge over a small stream through a wooded area called "Peckmill Bottoms" – note that it can get very muddy near the stream during the wetter months (photo below).

The route then joins a gravel track that leads up to the Dixon Drive residential estate in Chelford.

You then cross over the A537 onto Pepper Street for 500m before turning right onto the next off-road section through a wood known as "Stockin Moss", which is usually fairly firm but can become muddy in places during the winter. At the end of the path, the route turns right and then promptly left onto a narrow lane, which leads onto Sandhole Lane and then onto Moss Lane.

At the sharp right-hand bend, the waymarked route continues straight on into a field, but this is usually not navigable by bike, so this route continues along the road for a further 400m and then turns sharp left to follow a gravel track past a farm to re-join the waymarked route by the notable water tower (adjacent photo).

The route then continues along a path at the edge of a field (which can be a bit bumpy) and emerges by Colshaw Hall Country Estate and then joins Stocks Lane before turning left onto Grotto Lane.

When you reach a crossroads junction, the route turns right onto Blackden Lane, which leads past the driveway to Peover Hall, continues down to cross the Peover Eye stream and up the other side to reach a right turn onto the next section of off-road bridleway. This next section comprises 1km along a tree-lined single-track path and a further 1.4km along a farm track, both of which are slightly downhill, making for a fast and exhilarating ride – especially for the first part if you choose to pick up the pace and weave through the trees (photo below) - but mind the muddy patches if it's been wet!

The junction at the end leads onto Booth Bed Lane, which takes you to a junction that crosses the A50 onto Townfield Lane and a series of further quiet country lanes that lead onto another off-road section along Sandy Lane. This time, however, the gradient is upwards (but only slightly) and there are several gates to negotiate through a farmyard, plus a section of fairly bumpy cobbles. Around the half-way point of Sandy Lane, the surface becomes a bit smoother as it leads up to another junction with the A50.

This time, you join the A50 for 200m and then turn left onto Stocks Lane to pass by Barclays Bank at Radbroke Hall and Stocks Lane Nurseries before taking a left turn for more off-road riding. This section leads along a firm gravel track and emerges onto a road by Lower Moss Wood but then turns to follow a narrower path around more fields to reach a farm yard and a track that leads on to join Seven Sisters Lane towards Ollerton and the start of an on-road 2.5km section.

You cross directly over the A537 onto Marthall Lane, which drops down to cross Marthall Brook and up the other side to reach a left turn along a track that leads to an impressively-gated property (aka "Wayne's World"!). This section differs from the original route of the Cheshire Cheese Loop as the right of way has been changed and you need to bear right through a gate and follow the wire fence around to the other side of the property. The route then crosses over Pedley Brook, encounters a short sharp climb and continues to a 90-degree bend.

This is the point of intersection of the Cheshire Cheese Loop and the Heritage Loop – the Cheshire Cheese Loop turns right to return to its start-point in Warford; however, this route now turns left to join the Heritage Loop. The route continues alongside the edge of two fields and emerges onto a firm track that leads into the village of Mobberley via Damson Lane, which leads to Mill Lane and the picturesque adjacent Bulls Head and Roebuck pubs (the Roebuck opens for morning coffee if you fancy a stop).

The next 2.5km are along a series of lanes that cross the B5085, lead past the Church Inn to join Lady Lane, which leads to the second runway at Manchester Airport. The route then turns right and follows a gravel track (which can be muddy) to reach Ostler's Lane and onto Davenport Lane and a right turn onto Burleyhurst Lane (take care at the junction regarding fast-moving traffic coming around the bend).

The next off-road section is along Graveyard Lane, which leads onto more lanes and around past the Plough and Flail pub (opportunity for a cheeky drink?). Continue along the lane and then around to the left, which leads to more off-road on a gravel path and a swift downhill section (photo below) past the residential Lindow Court Park, emerging onto Moor Lane at the end.

More off-road soon follows with a left turn onto Rotherwood Road, which leads along the edge of Lindow Moss (photo below - spare a moment to think about poor Lindow Man), past the kennels and onto Eccups Lane, with a narrow path section leading down to Mossways Park residential estate.

The road then leads up to Morley Green, crosses Mobberley Road and follows Morley Green Road to the junction with the A538 for a steep descent to the River Bollin. It is advisable to stay on the footpath/cycle-path as you descend the hill to avoid the traffic - but take care of the kink in the path at the bottom by the bus stop. It is also advisable to dismount and cross the A538 via the islands at the bottom of the hill rather than at the waymarked sign opposite the hotel entrance.

41

The route then follows a path up towards the airport runway, which has a fairly steep but quite short climb that leads onto a wider gravel track next to the airport perimeter fence.

The track then heads away from the airport and joins Moss Lane for a mini-loop around the village of Styal, with a bit more off-road along Wilkins Lane before re-joining Altrincham Road to pass the Ship Inn and reach the junction with the B5166.

You then turn right and then right again onto Holt's Lane (the waymarked route follows the pavement for this short section) as the route heads into the National Trust property of Quarry Bank Mill (photo below). Follow the road on the approach to the mill and then either follow the waymarked signs just before the mill down a narrow, cobbled path with steps (not great unless on a MTB) or continue past the mill and cross over the next bridge over the river and loop back towards the first bridge.

This next section contains the only notable climb on the route, which is quite challenging if you are on a capable mountain bike and near-impossible on any other bike, owing to the combination of gradient, slippery surface and a series of steps to negotiate (photo below)

It does only last for around 200m so it's not too much of an ordeal to push your bike until you reach the gate at the top.

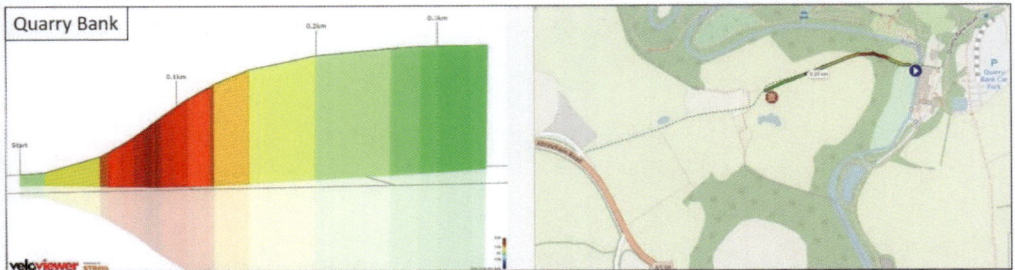

The path leads up to the busy A538, which requires crossing – head for the cycle path on the other side of the road, turn left and continue onto Nansmoss Road and then onto Mobberley Road. The following 2km retrace the outbound route back along Eccups Lane and past Lindow Moss to reach Moor Lane – here, the waymarked route heads down Cumber Lane to complete the loop, however this route follows Moor Lane, Chapel Lane and Alderley Road to return to the start-point in the centre of Wilmslow.

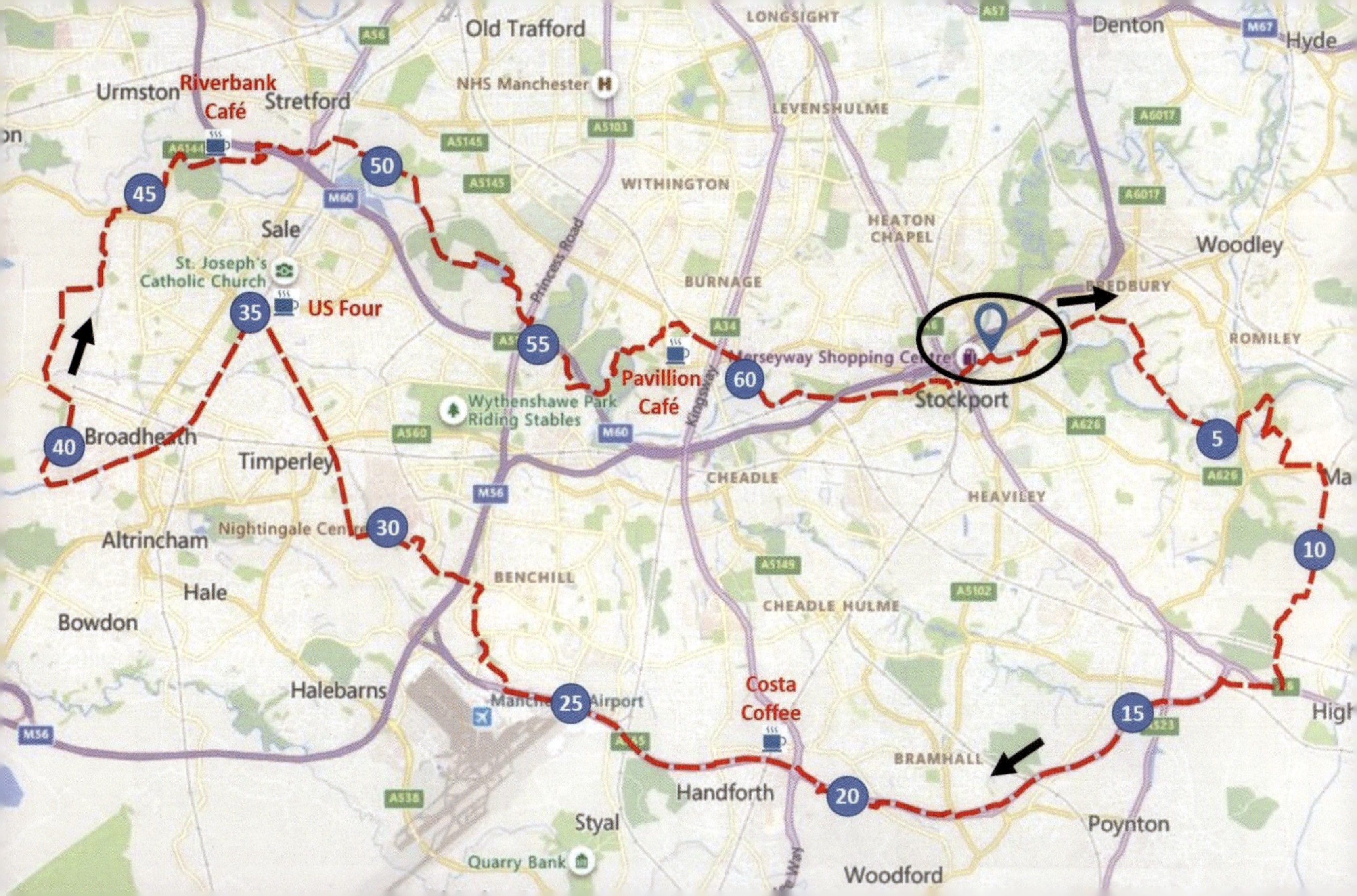
Old Trafford
Denton
Hyde
Urmston
Riverbank Café
Stretford
NHS Manchester
LONGSIGHT
LEVENSHULME
WITHINGTON
HEATON CHAPEL
Woodley
BREDBURY
ROMILEY
Sale
St. Joseph's Catholic Church
US Four
BURNAGE
Princess Road
Merseyway Shopping Centre
Pavillion Café
Kingsway
Wythenshawe Park Riding Stables
Stockport
Broadheath
Timperley
CHEADLE
HEAVILEY
Altrincham
Nightingale Centre
BENCHILL
Hale
Bowdon
CHEADLE HULME
Halebarns
Airport
Costa Coffee
BRAMHALL
Handforth
Styal
Poynton
Quarry Bank
Woodford
M60
M56
M67
A56
A57
A5103
A5145
A6017
A34
A560
A626
A5149
A5102
A523
A538
A555
A5144
5
10
15
20
25
30
35
40
45
50
55
60

6) MERSEY PARADISE

Dist. (km)	Elev. (m)	m/km	BC Index	Miles	Feet	Terrain
64.7	458	7.1	29.6	40.2	1503	5

Route Start-point: The Arden Arms (Millgate, Stockport)

Alternative Start-points: Rose Hill Station (Marple), Stanley Green, Brooklands, Sale Water Park

Stop-off Options: Costa Coffee (Stanley Green), US Four (Brooklands), Riverbank Café (Ashton on Mersey), Pavilion Café (Didsbury)

Ideal Bike: Gravel bike (ok on MTB but no technical features)

This is a route that links together sections of waymarked routes for almost all of its length, including Route 55 (with the Middlewood Way); the cycle path along the A555 airport link road; the Bridgewater Canal; and the Trans Pennine Trail (Route 62).

The Low-down on the Climbs

The elevation profile for the route is illustrated in the diagram below, highlighting the one notable climb.

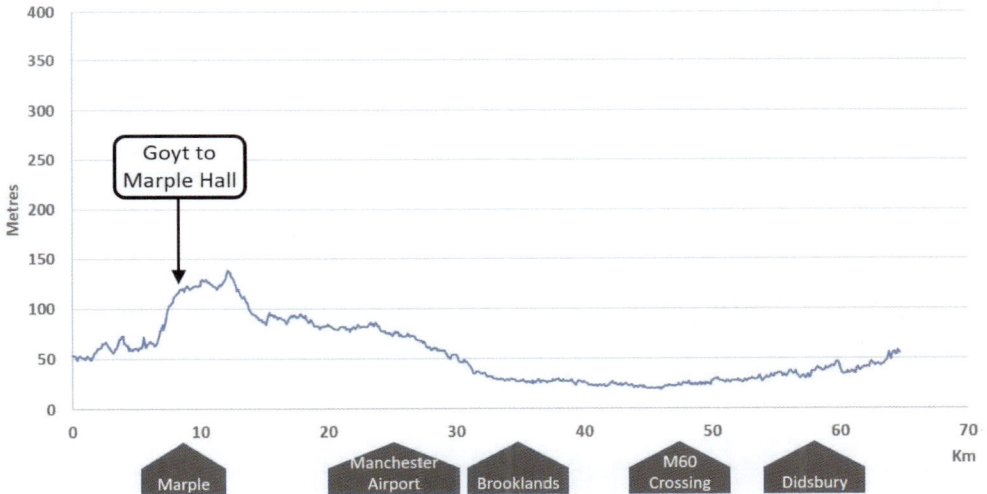

Climb	Distance (m)	Elevation Gain (m)	Peak Gradient	CBB Index	Features
Goyt to Marple Hall	1150	42	12%	10.0	Steep, tight and twisty!

Places of Interest on the Route

River Goyt and River Mersey

The River Goyt rises from near the Cat and Fiddle Inn and marks the old boundary between Cheshire and Derbyshire. It feeds into the Errwood and Fernilee Reservoirs before continuing to meet the River Dane to form the River Mersey in Stockport, which then flows to reach the Irish Sea at Liverpool.

Bridgewater Canal

This canal is managed by the Bridgewater Canal Company, which has a different cycling policy from the Canal and River Trust - cycling is only permitted on sections of renovated towpath, such as this route. The canal was opened in 1761, its success sparked the construction of rest of the UK's canal network.

Route Narrative

The start point of this route is the Arden Arms in Stockport - also used as a meeting place by the Stockport Clarion for their gravel and mountain bike rides. Stockport traces its history as far back as 1170, centred around a motte and bailey castle. In the 17th century, it was a centre of the hat-making industry - there is a museum in the town if you want to learn more.

This route departs in an easterly direction, following the cycle lanes along New Bridge Lane to reach Stockport Road West, which leads to National Cycle Route 55 with a right turn onto Osborne Street.

A right turn after a short distance takes you onto Dark Lane and the start of the first gravel section, which leads away from suburbia and into the countryside by the River Goyt. You then join the A627 for 200 metres before turning right by Chadkirk Business Park onto Vale Road, which leads down to a stunning bridge over the River Goyt with great scenery (photo below).

After crossing the river, you now face the only notable climb on the route, which snakes its way up through the trees on a gravel track to return to civilisation by Marple Hall School.

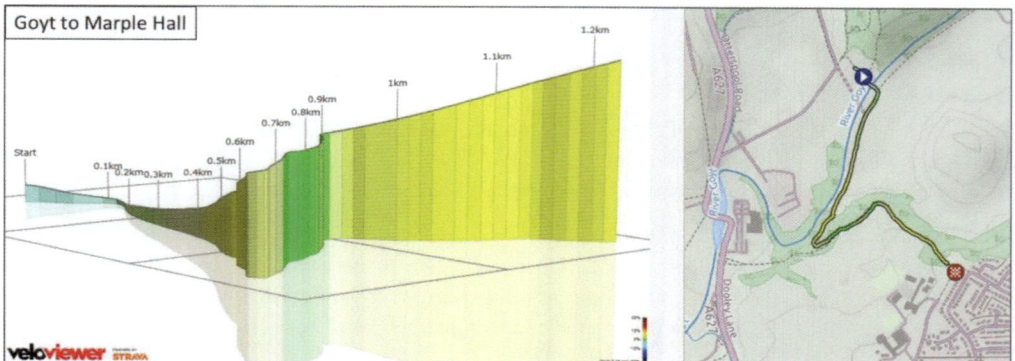

The route continues to follow Route 55 along a few residential streets to reach a Pelican crossing over Stockport Road that leads to Rose Hill train station. After you pass the car parking spaces you bear left onto the Middlewood Way, which has a mix of tarmacked and packed-gravel surfaces (photo below) - note that there are a few A-frame gates to weave through at the start of this section.

After 1.5km, you exit the Middlewood Way to the right and join Torkington Road, which leads onto Threaphurst Lane and up to a junction with the A6. After 350m, you bear left off the main road to join a section of the old main road that leads down to a spiral ramp onto the cycle path along the A555.

The route stays on the A555 cycle path for the next 13km, providing you with traffic-free cycling. Some of the cycleway is alongside the main road, with other sections that stray further to the side (photo below). Note that there are several junctions to cross along the way - all with Pelican crossings.

As you approach Manchester Airport, you bear left onto Enterprise Way, which leads onto Bailey Lane and then into Painswick Park (photo below) to join the Airport City Cycleway that leads you around the perimeter of Wythenshawe Hospital and onto Brooks Drive for a great section of single-track path to reach a busy roundabout junction with the A560.

Pick your way across the roundabout and continue along Brooklands Road, which continues in a straight line for 2.5km and delivers you to a ramp that leads down to the Bridgewater Canal (photo below).

After following the towpath for 4.5km, you leave the canal to the right onto Seamons Road, which then links up with the Trans Pennine Trail (TPT) - which now guides you for the rest of the route.

The initial section joins a series of single-track bridleways (photo below) to reach the River Mersey.

You cross the river and then follow the northern bank along more single-track paths for half a mile and then follow a trail through the woods that leads up to the M60. The route takes you on the bridge over the motorway (adjacent photo) and around the spiral ramp on the other side to then head east on more single-track.

You pass underneath the A56 and then underneath the Bridgewater Canal and the railway, following Hawthorne Road to return back to the northern bank of the river.

More bridleway sections then return you to the bank of the Mersey and lead to a fabulous trail around the scenic Chorlton Water Park.

The Mersey path leads you under Princess Parkway and onto a ramp that takes you up and over the river, you then follow a tarmacked cycle path that leads under Junction 5 of the M60. The TPT continues its meandering path eastwards, joining Ford Lane to pass under the motorway, then through Didsbury Golf Club, to cross back to the northern side of the Mersey and into Didsbury village.

The next section follows a path alongside the Manchester Metro and underneath the A6 by East Didsbury train station. The trail then leads back to the river as you make your way into Stockport town centre, passing back under the M60 and then over the river to join Chestergate.

You then cross King Street West to pass underneath the mighty train viaduct, built from 11 million bricks in 1839, and continue into the town centre along Great Underbank. A right turn then takes you onto Little Underbank and then Millgate, which leads you back to the Arden Arms.

7) BIDDULPH VALLEY WAY, RUDYARD AND BOSLEY CLOUD

Dist. (km)	Elev. (m)	m/km	BC Index	Miles	Feet	Terrain
51.0	645	12.6	32.9	31.7	2116	7

Route Start-point: Brook Street, Congleton

Alternative Start-points: Whitfield Valley, Morrisons (Leek), Rudyard Lake / Railway, Ruston Spencer

Stop-off Options: Starbucks (Smallthorne), Leek (lots of cafes), Platform 2 (Rudyard Railway)

Ideal Bike: Capable gravel bike or MTB (several technical sections around Bosley Cloud)

This route forms a fabulous circuit by virtue of the Biddulph Valley Way (Route 55), the Caldon Canal (Routes 550 and 559, Rudyard Lake Railway and a series of bridleways by Bosley Cloud. The vast majority of the route is easy terrain, but the section by Bosley Cloud contains a few stony trails that are great fun on a mountain bike and quite challenging on a gravel bike (depending on your skill and appetite!)

The Low-down on the Climbs

The elevation profile for the route is illustrated in the diagram below, highlighting the key climbs.

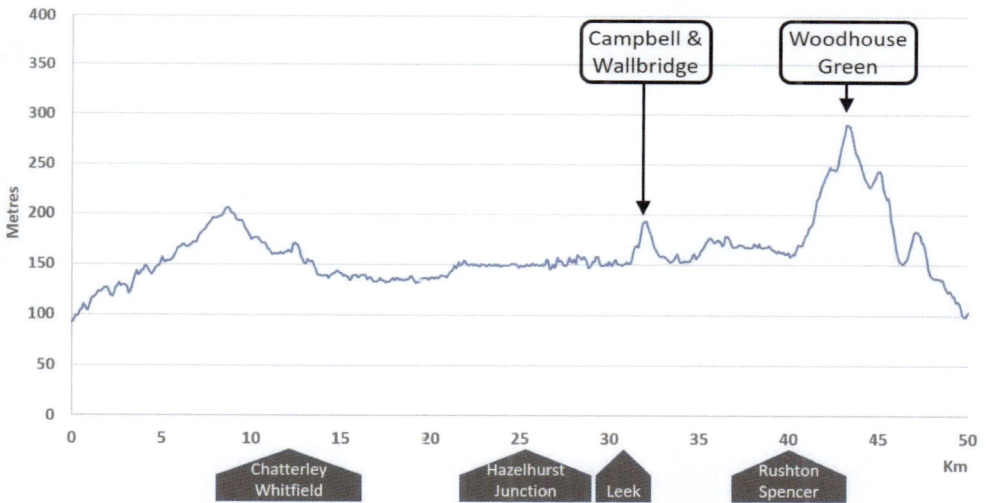

Climb	Distance (m)	Elevation Gain (m)	Peak Gradient	CBB Index	Features
Campbell & Wallbridge	700	40	12%	14.4	Fairly steep road climb
Woodhouse Green	2950	149	14%	20.6	Long road climb, steep in places

Places of Interest on the Route

Biddulph Valley Way (BVW)

Running along the course of the former Biddulph Valley Line, that was mainly used for the transport of coal, it is now a multi-user path that runs from Congleton down to the northern edge of Stoke-on-Trent.

Chatterley Whitfield

This was the largest coal mine in the area - producing over 1 million tons per year. It dates from around 1750 and ceased operation in 1977. There was a museum on the site but that closed in 1993. There are heritage open days that give an insight into the site's history.

Caldon Canal

This is a branch line off the Trent and Mersey canal that runs for 29km from Stoke to Froghall. The canal serves as the basis of Cycle Route 550 for the stretch between Stoke and Cheddleton.

Rudyard Lake & Railway

Rudyard Lake is a 3km-long reservoir that was built to maintain the water level of the Caldon Canal. The railway alongside served to bring visitors to the lake, including Rudyard Kipling's parents (hence his name!). The railway now operates as a 2.4km narrow gauge line with miniature steam trains.

Route Narrative

This route starts from the northern end of the Biddulph Valley Way (BVW), close to the centre of Congleton. The BVW forms part of National Cycle Route 55 and continues for the next 10km with a surface that varies from hard-packed gravel to tarmac (photo below).

Progress is largely uninterrupted for this section - apart from a few barriers to weave around. To the south of Biddulph, after Brown Lees Road, there is a section of narrow single-track path (photo below).

The BVW proceeds further south and crosses the A527 by means of a bridge over the main road, it then leads into Chatterley Whitfield Heritage Park, which offers a fantastic experience of smooth cycle paths and stunning scenery (photo below).

The great scenery continues as you head further south, crossing twice over Ford Green Brook and riding past Ford Green Lake.

As the surroundings become more suburban, you leave Route 55 and the BVW, continuing along a path to the side of the former railway for a further kilometre to reach Birches Head Road. At the junction, you turn left to cross over the railway line and the canal and then left again down the ramp that leads onto the towpath of the Caldon Canal.

The route then follows the canal for the next 9km, along a hard-packed towpath that offers more stunning scenery along the way (photo below).

When you reach Hazelhurst Junction, you cross over the canal and join the towpath on the Leek Branch, which crosses back over the main canal and heads north east towards Leek - on Cycle Route 559. Note that there is a canal tunnel along this section, which is bypassed by the towpath - this involves a flight of steps (you will need to carry your bike) and a steep slope down the other side to re-join the canal.

At the end of the canal, the route continues to follow Route 559 by joining Barnfield Road, which passes through an industrial area to reach Newcastle Road. You then cross the main road onto Campbell Avenue, which marks the start of the first notable climb of the ride. This is a climb of two halves, with a lull in the middle prior to joining Wallbridge Drive. The steepest part of the climb is towards the top as it reaches a gradient of 12%.

The route then descends the other side of Wallbridge Drive and joins Westwood Heath Road to continue the descent until you reach Oakwood Road, which leads onto the start of the next off-road section.

The next section of the ride lasts for 7km as it follows the path of the former section of the Churnet Valley Railway. It starts as hard-packed gravel track for 2km, which leads you to Rudyard Station and the start of the Rudyard Lake Steam Railway. Here, the train track and cycle path run side-by-side (photo below).

After you reach the end of the train line, the trail continues north through to Ruston Spencer - where you leave the old railway to the left onto Station Lane and approach the start of the other notable climb.

This climb lasts for almost 3km with 149m of elevation gain as you pass through Woodhouse Green and scale the eastern side of Bosley Cloud.

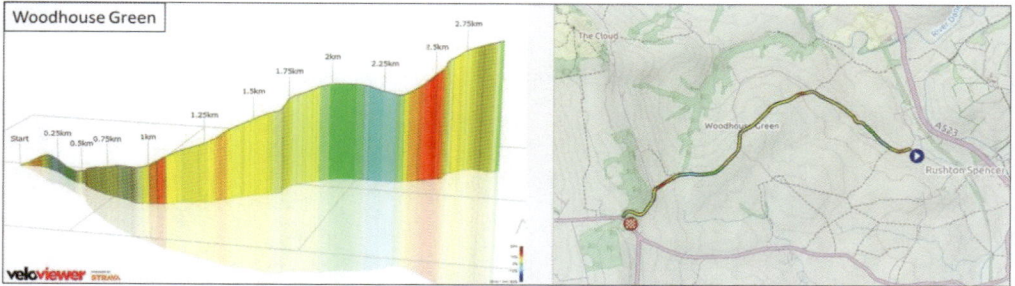

After you clear the top of the climb, the route descends and then takes a right turn onto Gosberryhole Lane, which starts on tarmac and then bears left onto a fabulous gravel track - descending initially and then climbing with a few technical features to negotiate. You then descend a steep, stony track to reach Tunstall Road and cross over to descend Acorn Lane - this is the most technical section of the route (photo below) - if you don't like the look of it then turn right on Tunstall Road to shortcut onto Under Rainow Road.

You then join Brookhouse Lane, which starts as tarmacked lane and then becomes a gravel track that runs parallel to the BVW and leads onto Bromley Road to return to the start.

8) COWN EDGE AND THE PEAK FOREST CANAL

Dist. (km)	Elev. (m)	m/km	BC Index	Miles	Feet	Terrain
43.5	806	18.5	35.1	27.0	2644	6

Route Start-point: Roman Lakes (Marple)

Alternative Start-points: Marple Bridge, Hayfield, New Mills, Chinley

Stop-off Options: Marple Bridge, Millies Tea Rooms (Hayfield), Sett Valley Café, New Mills, Tea On The Green (Chinley)

Ideal Bike: Great on either a Gravel Bike or MTB

This route takes you to the heights and viewpoints of the Cown Edge Bridleway (378m above sea-level); follows the fantastic Sett Valley Way (with a great café!); exposes you to the remoteness of Chinley Churn; and returns most of the way along the scenic Peak Forest Canal.

The Low-down on the Climbs

The elevation profile for the route is illustrated in the diagram below, highlighting the key climbs.

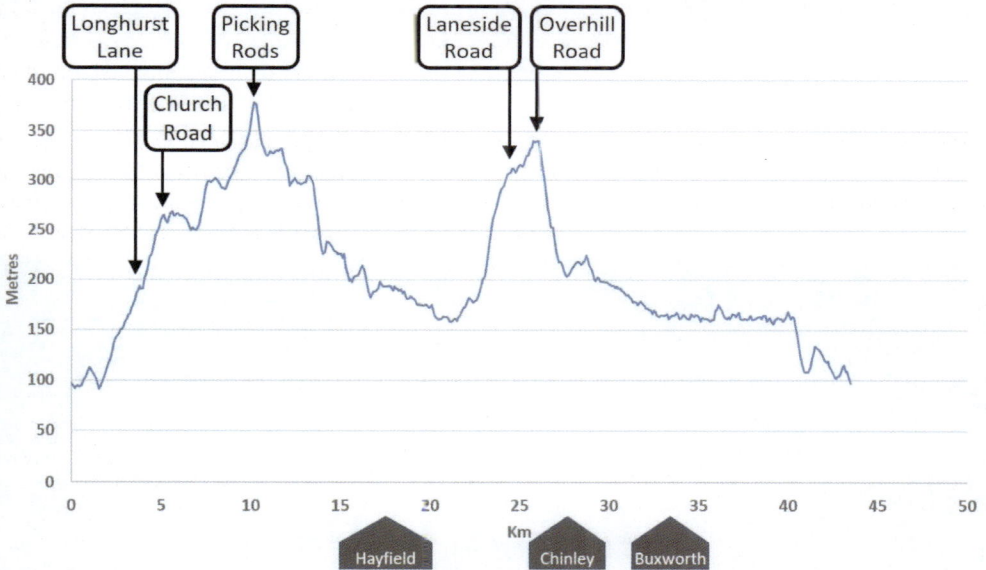

Climb	Distance (m)	Elevation Gain (m)	Peak Gradient	CBB Index	Features
Longhurst Lane	2300	99	10%	15.2	Fairly steep and narrow gravel climb, gets muddy when wet
Church Road	1200	89	13%	22.6	Starts steep on the road, then continues as gravel
Picking Rods	1600	86	11%	17.0	Gravel climb that starts shallow and steepens as it progresses
Laneside Road	1600	120	17%	25.6	Steep road climb
Overhill Road	1800	61	12%	10.6	Double-track gravel lane

Places of Interest on the Route

Roman Lakes
These lakes don't actually date from the Roman era but do trace their history back to 1086 and include a range of visitor attractions, including a café.

Cown Edge
This is a rocky ridge with a high point of 411m above sea level and offers great views.

The Sett Valley Trail
This is a 4km multi-user trail restored from the former New Mills to Hayfield branch line.

Peak Forest Canal
This canal runs from Whitelands Basin (the end of both the Huddersfield Narrow Canal and the Ashton Canal) to Whaley Bridge and Buxworth. It has a flight of 16 locks over the distance of a mile in Marple, where it also connects to the Macclesfield Canal.

Route Narrative

The start-point of this route is The Roman Lakes Leisure Park in Marple. The route departs to the north along Lakes Road to reach a short, sharp climb up Low Lea Road, which then drops down to join Longhurst Lane for the first notable climb of the ride - a road-climb for 2.3km with a fairly steady gradient.

There is a tiny lull in the ascent as you turn left onto Church Road - and then it's up again... initially on tarmac to reach a right turn onto a gravel track that continues the climb.

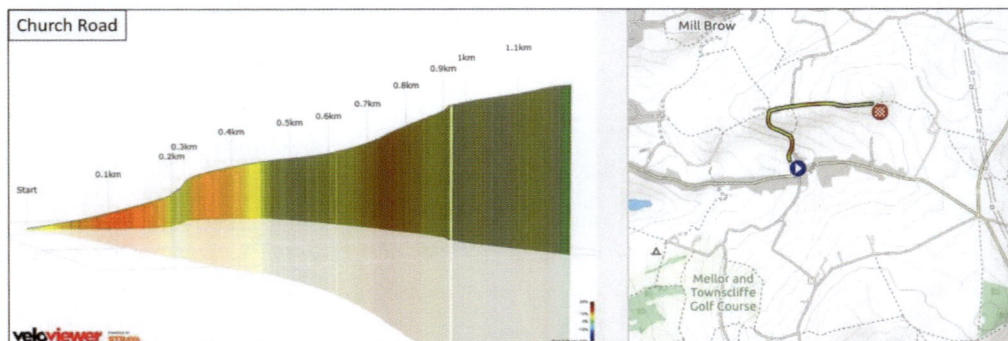

It's worth a pause when you reach the top to admire the views (photo below).

The route then emerges onto Shiloh Road to follow Route 68 for 2.5km - which also contains a short, sharp climb to reach over 300m above sea-level.

The right turn that follows takes you onto The Pennine Bridleway (PBW) - a 120-mile waymarked route through the Peak District and beyond. The first section is a gravel bridleway that leads past Robin Hood's Picking Rods (photo below), which probably originate from 10th century Saxon crosses but popular legend tells of Robin Hood using the stones for bending his bows.

The bridleway climbs with an easy gradient for most of the way but ramps up towards the top. The final 100m section is much steeper and rockier than the rest of the bridleway, so be prepared to finish the climb on foot (this final section is better suited for mountain bikes - but it is only for 100m).

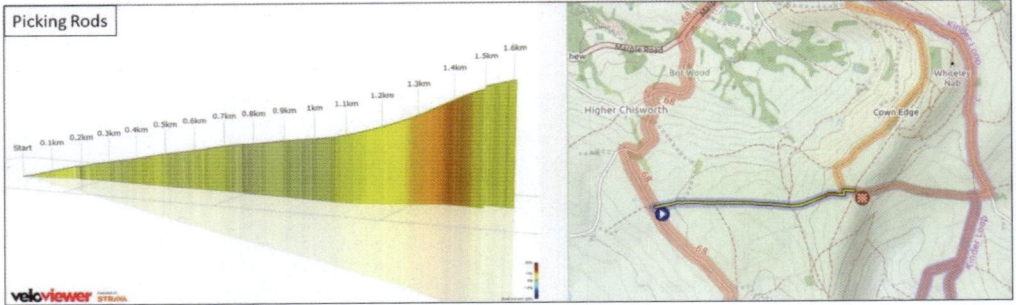

The descent on the other side is steep at the top with a loose surface, so proceed accordingly - but it soon flattens out if you decide to wheel your bike down the steep start. The surface also changes from gravel to tarmac as you progress.

A right turn keeps you on The Pennine Bridleway as you head south to reach a right-hand bend, after which you start to descend, go around a left bend and then take a left turn onto a double-width gravel track. The PBW continues around to the left and becomes a single-track path (photo below) with numerous rocks, stones and ruts to negotiate - but the gradient is flat and it is manageable on a gravel bike.

The route then leaves the PBW by taking a left turn through a farm - there are "Footpath Only" signs, so please wheel your bike through the farmyard and remount when you pass through the gate and join the tarmacked Lanehead Road.

You then descend swiftly to join the A624 for a kilometre and take a right turn onto Slack Lane, which leads to Primrose Lane for another stunning off-road single-track bridleway (photo below).

At the end of the trail, the route turns left and descends Swallow House Lane to pass underneath the A624 before looping round to cross back over it via a pedestrian crossing. You now join the Sett Valley Trail for the next 4km, which also features the fabulous Sett Valley Café if you wish to stop.

The Sett Valley Trail leads you to New Mills, where you turn off to the left, weave through residential streets and cross over the A6015 to join Laneside Road for an instalment of on-road climbing; it starts steady but ramps up to a gradient of around 17% for 0.3km in the middle before levelling out towards the top.

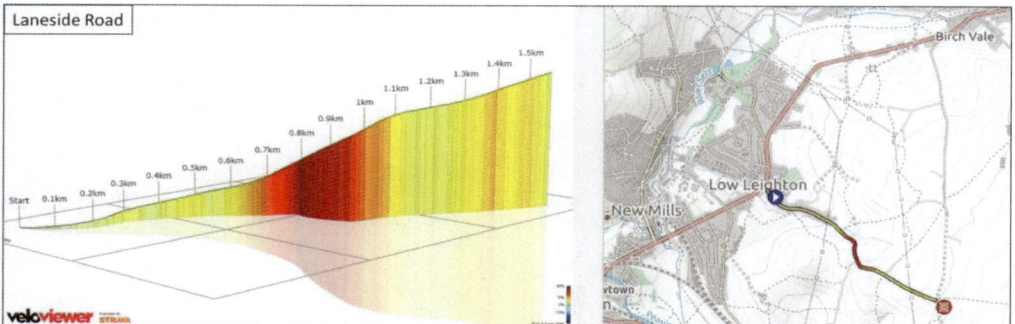

At the T-junction, the route turns right onto Overhill Road - a double-track gravel lane (photo below) that has a loose surface in places and is prone to puddles after wet weather.

The route then turns left at the end of the bridleway onto a tarmacked lane (still called Over Hill Road) that descends steeply to reach the village of Chinley. A right turn then leads over the railway and onto the B6062, which in turn leads onto the A624 for 200m before turning right onto Charley Lane.

Just before you reach the A6 flyover, the route turns right and joins the Peak Forest Tramway Trail, which was operational from 1796 until it was closed in 1924 - it was used for the transportation of limestone from the quarries in Dove Holes to the Peak Forest Canal in Buxworth. It is now a bumpy gravel track (photo below) - and ideal for gravel biking along (but does have a challenging surface in places).

At the end of the old tramway, you reach Buxworth Canal Basin (photo below) - once the largest and busiest inland port on the UK's canal network.

The route now continues along the towpath of the Peak Forest Canal, which has a surface of tarmac and hard-packed gravel along its length - but take care around the bridges as there are numerous potholes and sections of cobbles.

You stay on the towpath for around 8km, passing Furness Vale and New Mills to reach a flight of wooden steps that lead down to a double-track gravel lane that descends to meet the B6101. The route crosses the road onto Station Road, passes by the picturesque Dovecotes Lodge and joins the bridleway that leads back to The Roman Lakes (this used to be a fun rocky track for mountain biking but was levelled and filled in mid-2020).

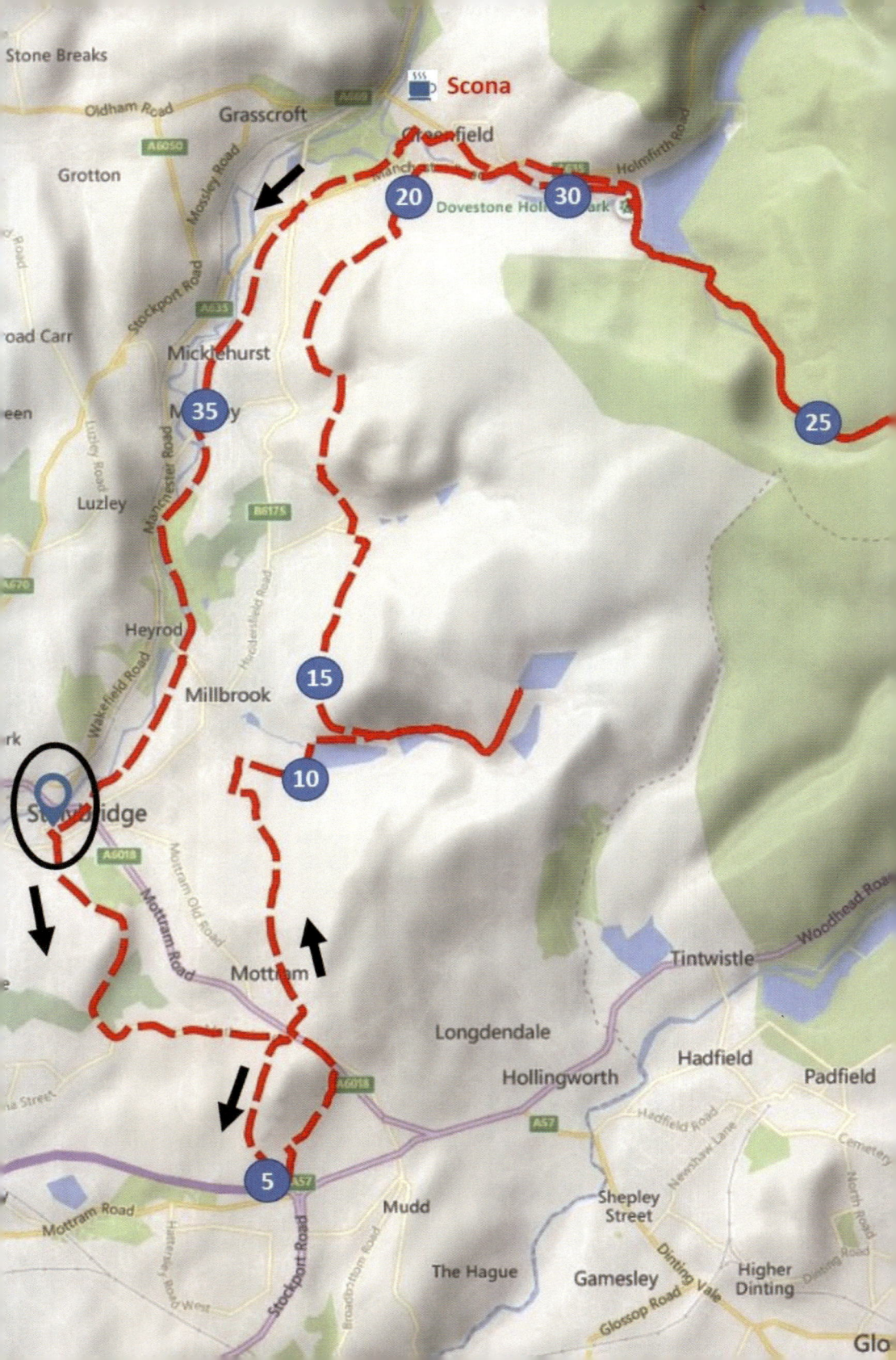

9) CHEWING GRAVEL

Dist. (km)	Elev. (m)	m/km	BC Index	Miles	Feet	Terrain
39.3	976	24.8	38.4	24.4	3202	7

Route Start-point: Tesco (Stalybridge)

Alternative Start-points: Greenfield, Dovestone Reservoir

Stop-off Options: Scona (The Greenfield Centre)

Ideal Bike: Hardtail MTB or capable gravel bike (the route comprises several technical sections)

Although this route measures less than 40km, it packs quite a punch with several demanding climbs and a number of technical sections. It also offers some amazing scenery along Chew Road.

The Low-down on the Climbs

The elevation profile for the route is illustrated in the diagram below, highlighting the notable climbs.

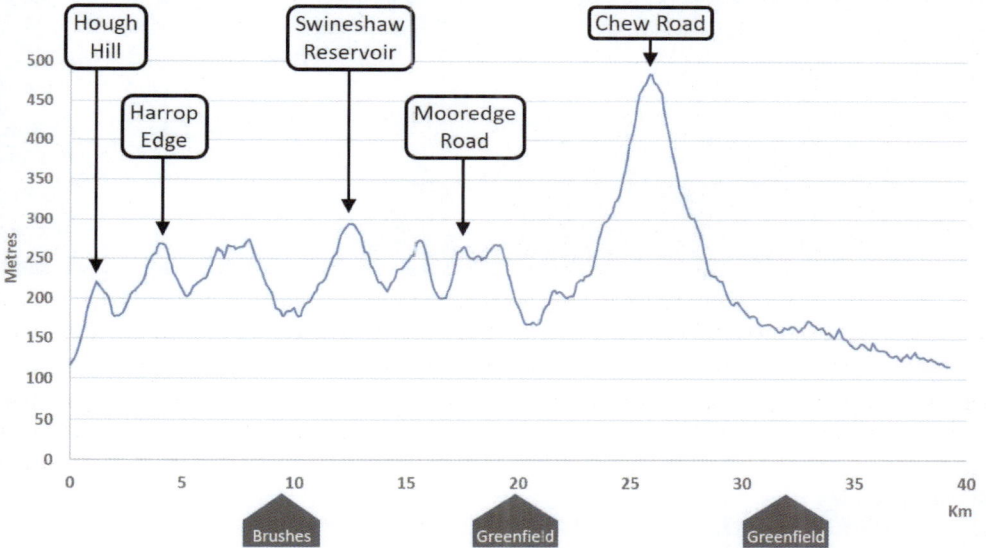

There are five notable climbs on this route, including the formidable Chew Road, their vital statistics are listed below.

Climb	Distance (m)	Elevation Gain (m)	Peak Gradient	CBB Index	Features
Hough Hill	600	65	21%	29.3	Very steep on-road, then becomes gnarly gravel
Harrop Edge	1800	93	11%	16.9	Steady road climb
Swineshaw Reservoir	1200	87	13%	22.0	Steep climb, loose in places
Mooredge Road	600	59	16%	26.1	Steep, technical off-road climb
Chew Road	4900	362	23%	46.4	Very demanding climb, with steep sections - some loose

Places of Interest on the Route

Brushes Valley Reservoirs

There are four connected reservoirs in the valley that hold a combined volume of 3.3 billion litres and provide drinking water for Greater Manchester.

Chew Valley Reservoirs

This is another group of four reservoirs; the largest is the lowest one - Dovestone, with a capacity of almost 5 billion litres. The area includes a nature reserve that is home to peregrine falcons.

Huddersfield Narrow Canal

This canal was opened in 1811 and runs for 32km from Huddersfield to Whitelands Basin in Ashton-under-Lyne. It boasts a total of 74 locks and has the longest canal tunnel in the UK at a length of 5.2km.

Route Narrative

This route starts as it means to go on... from Tesco, you head south and dog-leg right-left across the B6175 to join Hough Hill Road, which marks the start of the first notable climb of the ride.

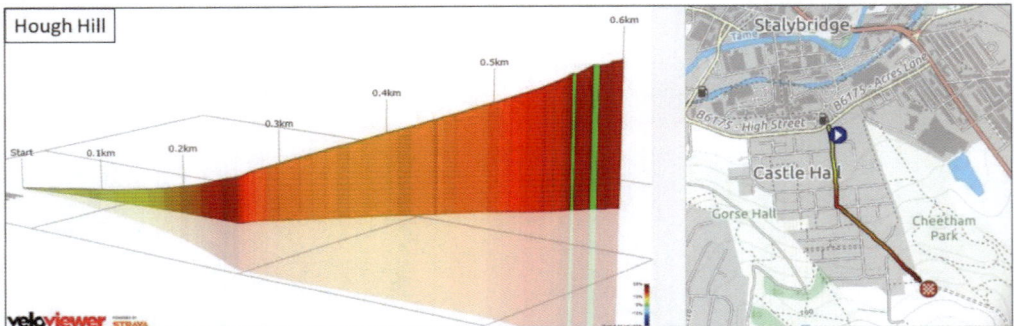

This climb ramps up in front of you along the residential streets of Castle Hall, peaking at the cobbled end of the street (you will need to scale the high kerb and cross over the pavement to re-join the road). As you reach the end of Hough Hill Road, you join a bridleway to complete the climb. This initial stretch of the bridleway is steep, loose and slippery; it was also quite washed-away when I last rode it (October 2020), so you may need to wheel the bike for a short distance - after which, the gradient lessens and the surface improves.

At the top, you pass through a gate and then have an exhilarating gravel descent all the way down to reach Early Bank Road - note that this section becomes muddy and slippery with deep puddles after long spells of wet weather.

A left turn then takes you onto Matley Lane by the Rising Moon pub to start the second climb of the ride, which is a road-climb that takes you close to the summit of Harrop Edge offering great views across to Manchester City Centre.

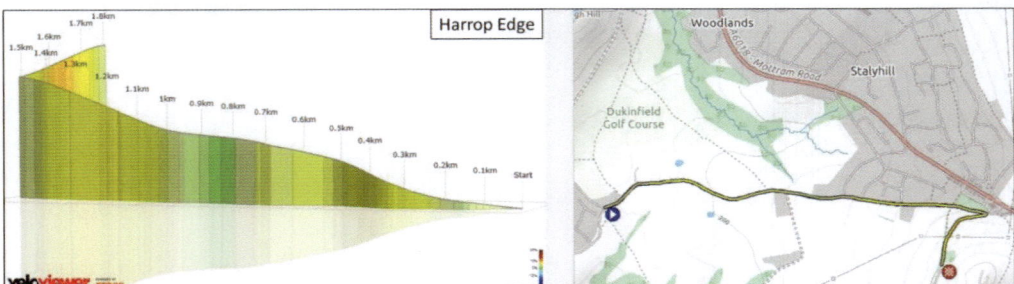

From the top of the climb, you start your descent along the road to reach a gate that leads onto a stony double-track bridleway- offering an exhilarating descent all the way down towards the main roundabout junction at the end of the M67 motorway. On reaching the road at the bottom of the descent, you then turn immediately left onto another bridleway that leads through a gate and through a farmyard. You then reach a row of trees and turn left to follow a track that climbs through the trees (photo below).

After the trees, you bear right onto a double-track gravel path and continue upwards (with great views to the right) to reach the A6108. A left turn takes you onto the main road for 0.4km before you turn right onto a short, sharp, cobbled climb up Gallowsclough Road to reach the next off-road section.

The initial part of this section can be very wet until you reach a gate by a farm, after which the track becomes a gritty section of single-track - offering a fabulous descent (photo below) to reach Flaxfield Farm before emerging onto a housing estate.

The route then takes a right onto Brushes Road that leads around to the dam-end of Walkerwood Reservoir, which offers a great viewpoint. You then continue around to the right to reach a gate, where you bear left and commence the start of the next climb - one of the less intense ones from Simon Warren's Cycling Climbs of North West England - up to Higher Swineshaw Reservoir.

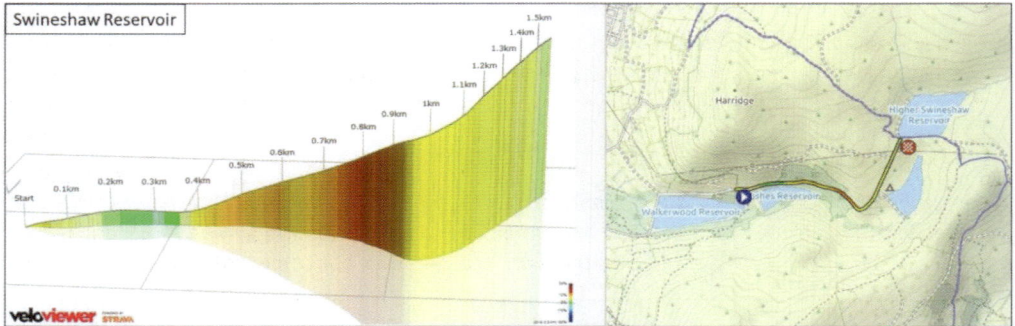

The climb has a gradual start as you pass by Brushes Reservoir and then ramps up to a gradient of around 13% until you reach a left-hand bend - note that the surface can have a layer of gravel to add to the challenge. After the bend, the gradient eases and you continue past Lower Swineshaw Reservoir all the way to the end of the straight (mind the drainage channels) to reach an amazing view across the upper reservoir (photo below - taken in summer 2018 after the moorland fires).

You then retrace the route back down (mind the loose gravel) until you reach the gate, whereby you take the bridleway on the right.

The following 6km section of the route follows the Pennine Bridleway (PBW) and is quite technical, with loose stones and rocks to negotiate - as well as a few steeper sections of climb and descent. The first section is a punchy climb that is littered with fist-sized stones (photo below).

After the initial ramp, the gradient eases and you continue along before dropping steeply to return to tarmac briefly along Castle Lane.

As the route leaves the tarmac, you commence the next climb up Mooredge Road - this is a demanding climb as its surface is steep, loose and stony - if you dare to break your concentration, you can try to spot the remains of Buckton Castle on your right.

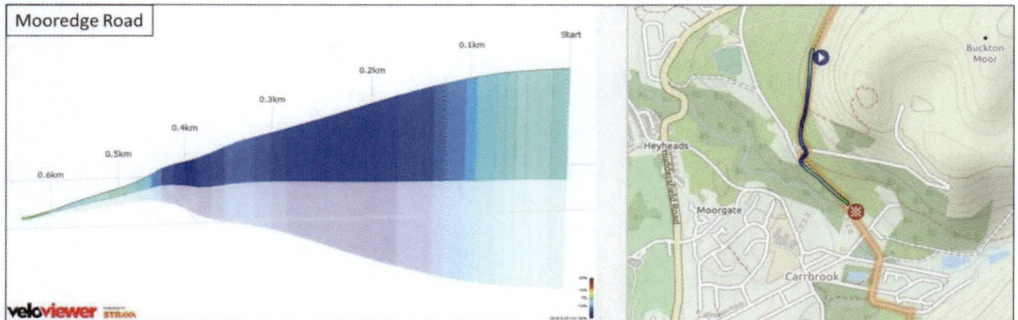

The next 2km remain on the level as you continue to progress north to reach a cluster of houses at the end of the gravel track. You then descend and join Friezland Road, which ends at a junction with the A635.

A right turn leads to a roundabout, which marks the start of one of the more monstrous climbs of North West England - another one from Simon Warren's collection, this one scoring 8/10.

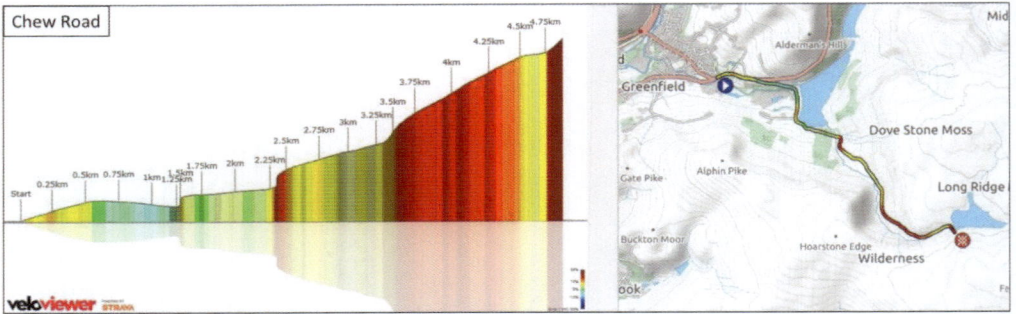

The climb starts from the roundabout with a steady incline on the main road to reach the entrance to Dovestone Reservoir. You then descend briefly before reaching a short, sharp section of climb that rises to the level of Dovestone Reservoir and its sailing club.

After clearing the reservoir, the route crosses a bridge over a stream and bends around to the right to commence the main section of the climb - be prepared to dig deep for the next 2.7km as you make your way up through the valley alongside Chew Brook. There are several gates to pass through that may require a dismount. The surface varies between tarmac and loose gravel - the incline pitches as well - sometimes combining steep gradient with a loose surface - made even tougher if there is a headwind!

The reward for your efforts on reaching the top are the stunning views - across Chew Reservoir and also down the valley (photo below). The descent is great fun but stay alert with the loose surface and give yourself plenty of time to stop for the gates.

When you reach the sailing club, the route bears left and follows a lower gravel lane alongside the brook to emerge back at the A635 roundabout. Here, you go over the roundabout onto Chew Valley Road, which leads Ladhill Lane and onwards to join the Saddleworth Linear multi-user path.

You follow the trail heading south to reach its end in Mossley, where you emerge onto Egmont Street and then turn onto the towpath of the Huddersfield Narrow Canal. After almost 1km on the towpath, you enter a 150m tunnel - it is safer to wheel your bike through the tunnel as the surface is of broken cobbles (photo below) - it also gets very dark if you don't have lights!

At Grove Road, you leave the canal and follow the picturesque Yellow Brick Road trail (photo below) to reach the outskirts of Stalybridge. The final section of the route takes you back onto the canal to skip the busy Mottram Road junction and delivers you back to the start in the town centre.

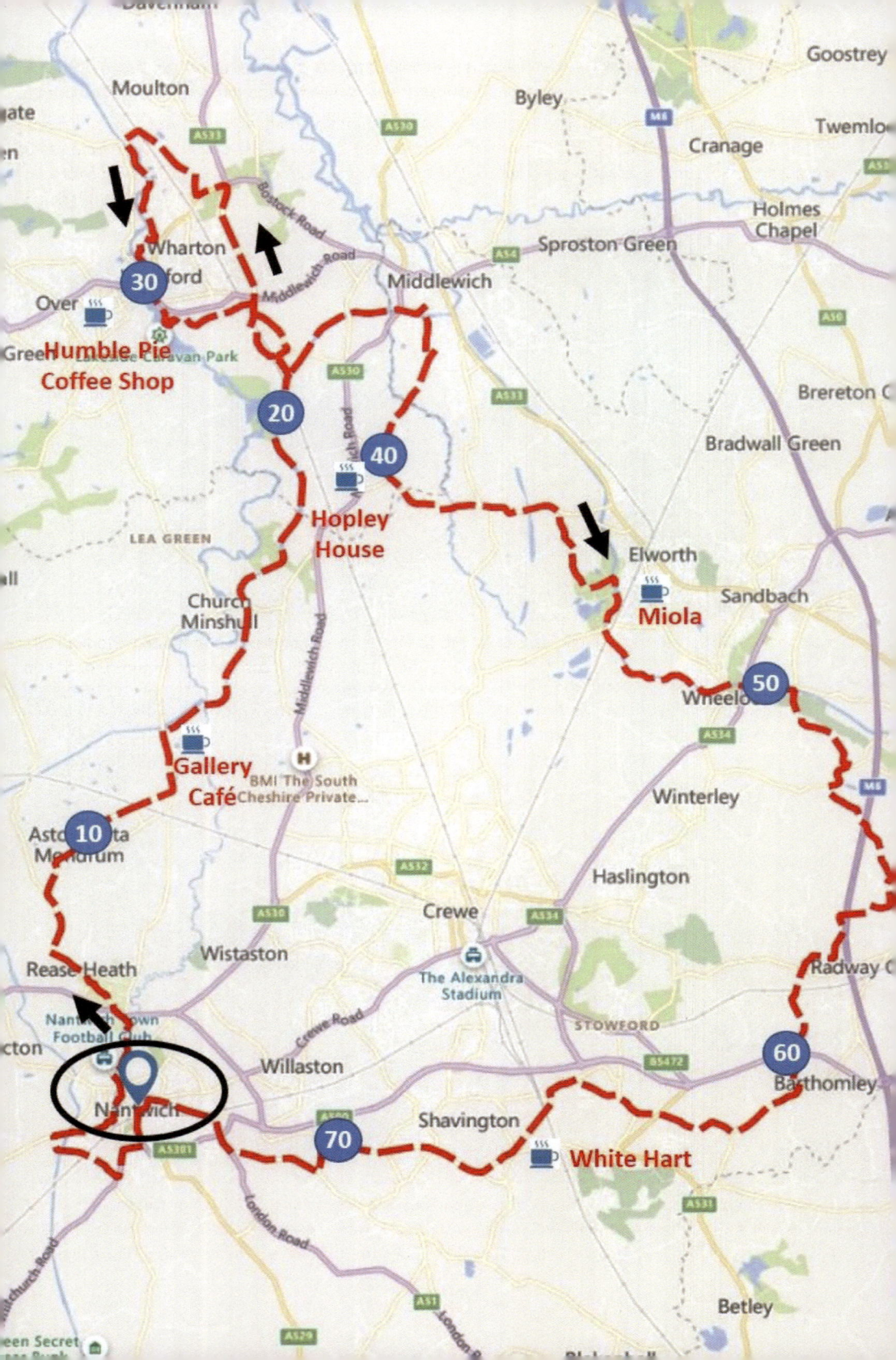

10) NANTWICH CANAL-FEST

Dist. (km)	Elev. (m)	m/km	BC Index	Miles	Feet	Terrain
74.4	519	7.0	38.6	46.2	1703	5

Route Start-point: Nantwich Train Station

Alternative Start-points: Winsford, Middlewich, Alsager

Stop-off Options: Gallery Café (Aqueduct Marina), Humble Pie (Winsford), Hopley House (Nantwich Road), Miola (Sandbach), White Hart (Hough)

Ideal Bike: Great on either a Gravel Bike or MTB

This route includes a lot of canal towpath - some on smooth surfaces, some on rougher paths, it also includes two great sections along the River Weaver: one in Nantwich and another fab one by Winsford.

The Low-down on the Climbs

There is negligible climbing on this route, as illustrated by the elevation profile below.

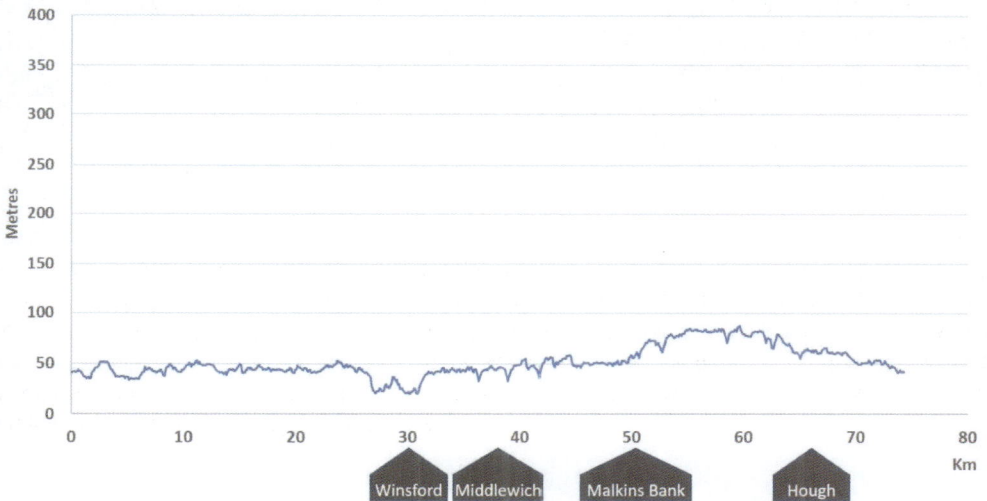

Places of Interest on the Route

Nantwich
This town's history stems from its salt production, dating from Roman times. It now boasts the highest concentration of listed buildings in England.

River Weaver
This river runs for over 80km from the Mid-Cheshire Ridge to the Mersey Estuary at Weston Point (near Runcorn). It is navigable from Winsford and includes several locks. One of its most notable features is the Anderton Boat Lift that connects the river with the Trent and Mersey Canal.

Shropshire Union Canal
This canal starts in Wolverhampton and provides a link between the canals of the West Midlands up to the Manchester Ship Canal at Ellesmere Port. The canal has a "main line" (from Wolverhampton through to Ellesmere Port) and additional "branch lines" such as the Llangollen and Middlewich Canals.

Winsford Salt Mine
The mine was opened in 1844, it reaches a depth of almost 200m, has over 250km of tunnels, supplies most of the salt used for UK road-gritting and has a controlled storage facility covering 1.8 million m²!

Route Narrative

The route heads south out of Nantwich along Wellington Road, turns right onto Park Road and passes by Nantwich Lake. After you cross the river, you take a right turn onto the waymarked Weaver Way path, which follows a gravel track across a field (photo below).

After passing through a gate, the track continues and leads to an unmanned level crossing over a train line (take care whilst crossing!). You then follow a single-track path in a westerly direction that links up with a tarmacked lane to cross the canal and emerges onto Marsh Lane for a right turn.

The route now picks up Cycle Route 551 to cross back over the canal and turn right onto Queen's Drive. A further right turn takes you onto a cycle path that leads down to the River Weaver for a scenic section along the river and through a park (photo below).

Route 551 then crosses over the river and re-joins the road onto Waterlode through Nantwich before bearing left away from the road and back onto the riverside path for a further kilometre. You can ride on the pavement around the A51 roundabout and then cross the main road at the Pelican crossing to enter the grounds to Reaseheath College (if the college grounds are closed, then you can skip this section by continuing further along the main road and taking the next right turn).

Follow the route along the gravel paths through the college and turn right after the college onto Wettenhall Road for 2km. Dairy Lane ther leads onto the B5074, which takes you to the Middlewich Branch of the Shropshire Union Canal for the next instalment of off-road riding.

This section of towpath lasts for 7.5km and is very rural in nature - it doesn't get a lot of use and can be hard-going in places (depending on your bike), as shown in the photo below.

Just as the towpath improves, it's time to leave the canal (you will return later in the ride) with an exit onto Cycle Route 71, which has a short off-road section that leads onto Clive Back Lane. You then cross the A54 and proceed through Winsford Industrial Estate. A left and right turn takes you onto Smokehall Lane that becomes a single-track path through farmland. At the end, you turn left to pass underneath the railway and follow a tarmacked path to reach the Weaver Way, which provides a tarmacked path that follows the river into Winsford (photo below).

There is then a complicated junction to negotiate at Wharton Road Roundabout that involves crossing the river to cross the road and then a crossing back over the river before following a path that passes underneath the roundabout. The Weaver Way then takes you through the trees and around Rilshaw Meadows, looping around and climbing up to join Rilshaw Lane, which links up with Clive Lane and leads back to the canal where you left off.

You follow the canal for a further 2.5km and exit, following Route 71 through the streets of Middlewich but stay on Sutton Lane as it leaves the town and turns from tarmac into a fabulous gravel track (photo).

At the end of the track, you turn left and then left again to join Forge Mill Lane, which leads you onto National Cycle Route 5. The route then follows more rural lanes on Route 5 to reach the Trent and Mersey Canal in Ettiley Heath. You join the towpath on the western side of the canal, which starts with a good surface (photo below) but reverts to a bumpy track as you progress further.

When you reach Malkins Bank, you leave the towpath and follow a bridleway through the golf course to reach Mill Lane. The route now joins the Cheshire Cycleway (Route 70) and heads over the M6 via an off-road track - note that it can get very muddy after wet weather (photo below).

You return to tarmac on Nursery Road and continue on the Cheshire Cycleway for a total of 13km, weaving through the country lanes and crossing the train line just to the south of Oakhanger via another unmanned level crossing (photo below).

From Hough, you leave the Cheshire Cycleway and follow a combination of Newcastle Road and Wybunbury Lane to return to Nantwich.

11) TATTON PARK AND THE TPT TO RUNCORN

Dist. (km)	Elev. (m)	m/km	BC Index	Miles	Feet	Terrain
84.2	636	7.6	53.6	53.2	2087	5

Route Start-point: Tatton Park

Alternative Start-points: Dunham Massey, Stockton Heath, Runcorn, Acton Bridge, Arley Hall

Stop-off Options: Dunham Massey Ice Cream, Runcorn (lots), Davenport's Tea Room (Acton Bridge), Arley Hall, High Legh Garden Centre

Ideal Bike: Gravel bike (MTB ok - but no technical features)

This route mixes together the grounds of three country houses (Tatton Park - photo below, Dunham Massey and Arley Hall); 25km of the Trans Pennine Trail (TPT); a beautifully-surfaced section of the Bridgewater Canal and a fabulous section of Route 5 through Aston to create a fabulous route.

Places of Interest on the Route

Tatton Park

Tatton Park comprises a 1,000-acre deer park (with plenty of close-encounter opportunities - see photo), a neo-classical mansion, landscaped gardens, a medieval hall and a rare-breeds farm. The park hosts a wide range of events every year, including concerts and was a stage finish for the 2016 Tour of Britain. There is also a gift shop, a restaurant and a café.

Dunham Massey

Dunham Massey covers around 200 acres and is also home to a herd of deer. The hall was built in 1616 and there is an 18th century obelisk.

Manchester Ship Canal

The Ship Canal was opened in 1894 and established the "Port of Manchester" - connecting Salford Quays to the Irish Sea via a 58km waterway. At the peak of its construction it supported the employment of 17,000 people. It will support a ship of a maximum length of 530 feet with a height restriction of 70 feet.

Arley Hall

This is a Grade II listed building constructed in the 1830s set in impressive gardens. The hall and gardens are open to visitors and there is also a café.

St Helens (Sankey) Canal

This was Britain's first canal, opened in 1757 to transport coal from Haydock Collieries.

The Low-down on the Climbs

The elevation profile for the route is illustrated in the diagram below, there is one notable climb.

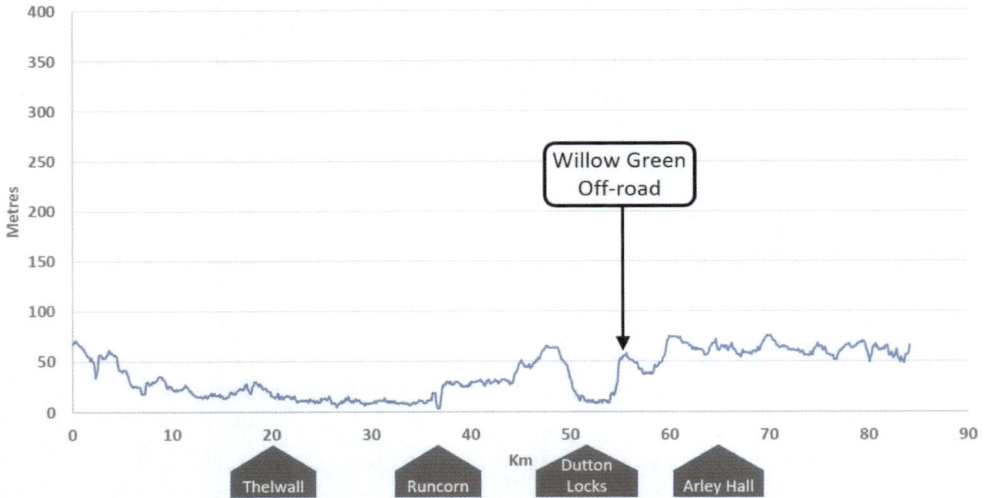

Climb	Distance (m)	Elevation Gain (m)	Peak Gradient	CBB Index	Features
Willow Green Off-road	600	37	12%	15.2	Fairly steep and narrow gravel climb, gets muddy when wet

Route Narrative

You start the route from the centre of Tatton Park and head north along Rostherne Avenue to leave the park grounds via the Rostherne Entrance/Exit. You then continue north through the village of Rostherne, with its 12th century church, to reach a junction with Chester Road. This was the old main road prior to the bypass, you proceed across Chester Road and then go up-and-over the bypass along a scenic country lane.

The route then passes underneath the M56 and rises back up to arrive at a junction onto the A56. A left-right manoeuvre then takes you onto Park Lane, which leads down to the Swan With Two Nicks pub and a narrow footbridge (adjacent photo) over the River Bollin.

Once over the river, you follow a gravel track around the western side of Dunham Massey that brings you out on Woodhouse Lane. A right and left turn then takes you through Dunham Town, over the Bridgewater Canal and onto a track that leads down to the Trans Pennine Trail (TPT).

This section of the TPT provides a wide, smooth-rolling gravel-surfaced trail that forms the basis of the route for the following 25km (photo below). Please be aware that the TPT can get busy with other users, so ride respectfully. There are also several roads that you will need to cross along the way.

As you approach Thelwall, you descend on the trail to reach a junction at the end with Bradshaw Lane, which leads onto the B5157 (Thelwall New Road). Turn left and follow the road alongside the Manchester Ship Canal to reach the busy junction with the A50. A right turn then takes you over the Latchford Swing Bridge, which is followed by a left turn (following the TPT waymarkers) onto a single-track trail by the side of the ship canal.

At the end of this section, you reach a junction with the A49, cross over and then follow another single-track trail alongside the canal that emerges in a residential area, where the path becomes tarmacked and leads to the A5060. A left and right turn leads onto Taylor Street and then Eastford Road, which turns from tarmac to gravel along its length and takes you on a meandering tour of canals, rivers and railways to reach the towpath of the St. Helens Canal - a fabulous, scenic stretch of gravel (photo below)!

The route follows the canal for almost 8km, which leads to the Mersey estuary by Widnes and the next highlight of the ride - the crossing of the Silver Jubilee Bridge over the Mersey - enjoy the views!

From the southern end of the bridge, the route joins the western end of the Bridgewater Canal and heads east around the perimeter of Runcorn - following the waymarked Runcorn Loop. This is another great section of towpath with a well-maintained surface (photo below).

You stay on the towpath for 6.5km and continue on the Runcorn Loop as it leaves the canal and proceeds through a residential area. After riding through a wooded area, you pass underneath the M56 and join Aston Lane South, which leads onto Route 5 and magnificent gravel descent (photo) to Dutton Locks.

From the locks, you stay on the northern side of the River Weaver and follow the tarmacked riverside path to reach the A49 by the Acton Bridge swing bridge. Here, you cross directly over the road and proceed along Willow Green Lane. The next feature of the ride is its only climb, which starts on the road as you climb over the canal and then continues off-road up a single-track path to emerge onto Leigh Lane.

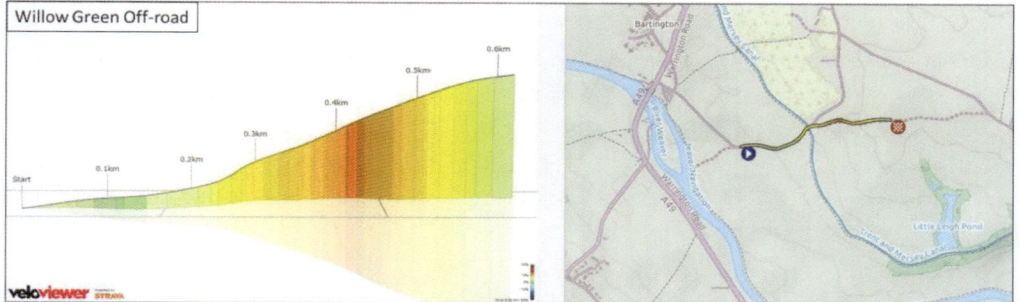

A series of country lanes takes you through Frandley and Antrobus, bringing you to a bridleway that leads you into the grounds of Arley Hall. This is a really interesting section of varying off-road surfaces, with paths, grass and fields that takes you past the main entrance to the Hall and around Back Lane for a bridleway exit from the estate - with more great riding on a range of surfaces (photo below).

After crossing over the M6 and another off-road section, the route returns to tarmac and follows a loop of lanes to reach more off-road with a bridleway through a farm that brings you back to Chester Road (the former A556). Yet another gravel track then sends you east in the direction of Knutsford to make your way down through the town park and out onto Mobberley Road.

A left turn then leads down to Mallard Close, which in turn leads over the railway line and to a gated entrance into Tatton Park. This alternative entrance to Tatton Park includes a 2km gravel track that passes around the eastern side of Tatton Mere and joins up with the main Knutsford Drive to return to the start.

12) MACC FOREST MONSTER

Dist. (km)	Elev. (m)	m/km	BC Index	Miles	Feet	Terrain
49.3	1302	26.4	64.2	30.6	4272	6

Route Start-point: Macclesfield Forest Visitor Centre

Alternative Start-points: Tegg's Nose, Pott Shrigley, Taxal, Goyt Valley, Cat and Fiddle Inn

Ideal Bike: Great on either a Gravel Bike or MTB (majority of off-road sections drain well)

Stop-off Options: Tegg's Nose Tearooms, Farm Made Tearooms, Goyt Valley ice cream van, Peak View Tearooms

This is the most demanding route in the book, packing-in over 1300m of climbing in under 50km - but it does offer amazing scenery and reaches 517m above sea-level at The Cat and Fiddle Inn.

The highlights of the route include riding through both sides of Macclesfield Forest; climbing a section of The Gritstone Trail up to Bowstones; and a fantastic tour through The Goyt Valley.

The Low-down on the Climbs

The elevation profile for the route is illustrated in the diagram below, highlighting the key climbs.

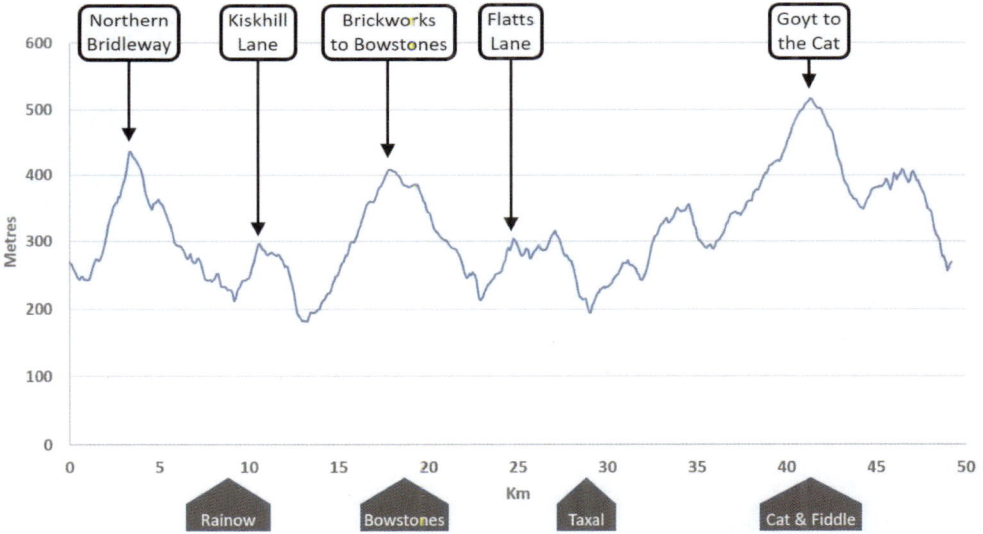

There are five notable climbs, including one Black, on this route, their vital statistics are listed below.

Climb	Distance (m)	Elevation Gain (m)	Peak Gradient	CBB Index	Features
Northern Bridleway	1400	116	25%	27.6	Steady climb that steepens towards the top
Kiskhill Lane	450	58	20%	33.7	Short but steep
Brickworks to Bowstones	3750	205	11%	25.9	Steady road climb for initial 3km, then gravel to the top
Flatts Lane	600	46	16%	19.5	Narrow, winding, steep and loose
Goyt to the Cat	5600	243	11%	24.8	Very scenic road climb, steepens towards the top

Places of Interest on the Route

Macclesfield Forest

Once covering an area of 50,000 acres in the Middle Ages, the forest now covers a mere 1,000 acres and rises to a peak elevation of 475m above sea-level. It also contains two reservoirs and supports a wide diversity of wildlife, including a large heronry.

The Goyt Valley

This valley lies to the south of Whaley Bridge and comprises Fernilee and Errwood reservoir that were constructed in the 20th century to supply drinking water to Stockport. The flooding of the valley to fill the reservoirs marked the end of the once-thriving community of farms, a school and a gunpowder factory.

Route Narrative

The route departs from the Macclesfield Forest Visitor Centre, descends around Ridgegate Reservoir to reach The Leather's Smithy pub and then take a sharp right turn onto Charity Lane. The route follows the road for 500m and takes a left through a gate onto the way-marked "Forest Bridleway" for the first climb.

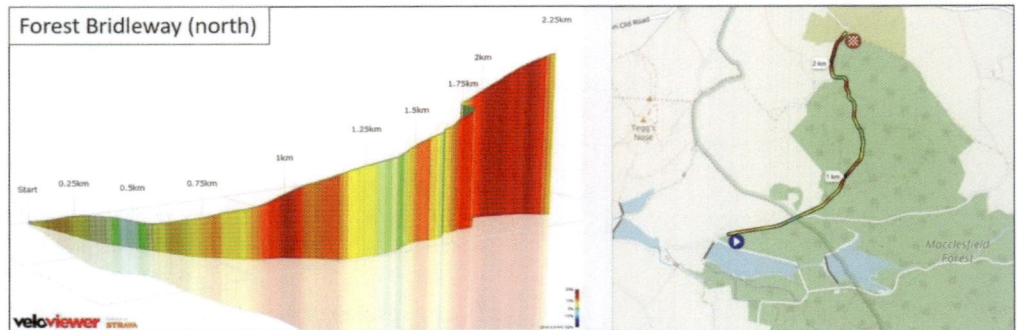

This climb has a gravel surface on a double-track path that winds through the northern part of the forest (photo below). It starts gently, steepens towards the middle and then really ramps up to around 25% gradient towards the end of the trail. If that wasn't enough, there is then a further 350m-long section of really steep (20%) road-ascent to the top of Hacked Way Lane to overcome to complete the climb.

The next off-road section follows a right turn just before Tegg's Nose Visitor Centre. This time is straight down the hill, which is not too steep but it is bumpy in places.

More descending follows along a series of lanes to reach Kiskhill Lane for another dose of climbing. The road surface is poor for a lane but not that of a bridle path, it is also steep - reaching 20% gradient.

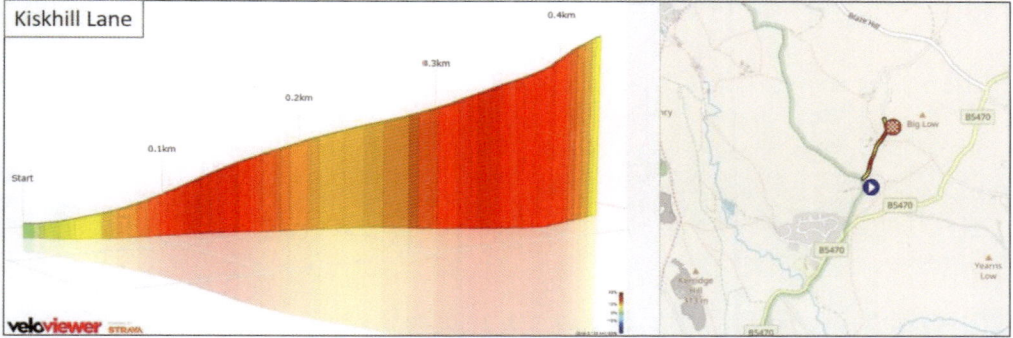

Kiskhill Lane leads onto Jumper Lane, which in turn leads to a left turn onto Blaze Hill, where you descend and can pick up a lot of speed - but be mindful of the impending right turn at the bottom onto Spuley Lane, which leads towards Pott Shrigley. From Pott Shrigley, the route joins Bakestonedale Road - otherwise known as "The Brickworks" - a favourite climb for many local events.

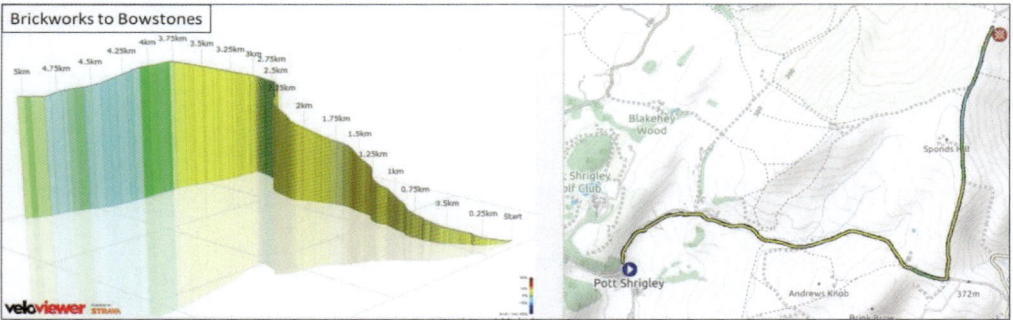

But this route delivers an extra punch, as from the top of the road climb, you take a left turn onto the Gritstone Trail and continue upwards on a gravel track (photo) that eventually leads to Bowstones Farm.

From Bowstones, the route descends along the road to reach Higher Lane for a right turn and a steep descent that leads to a left turn just after the sharp left corner, which leads further down and then back up again on a rural lane to reach the village of Kettleshulme.

You then cross over the B5470 onto Flatts Lane, which leads around to the next notable climb - a steep gravel track that heads up past Clayton Fold Christmas Tree Farm.

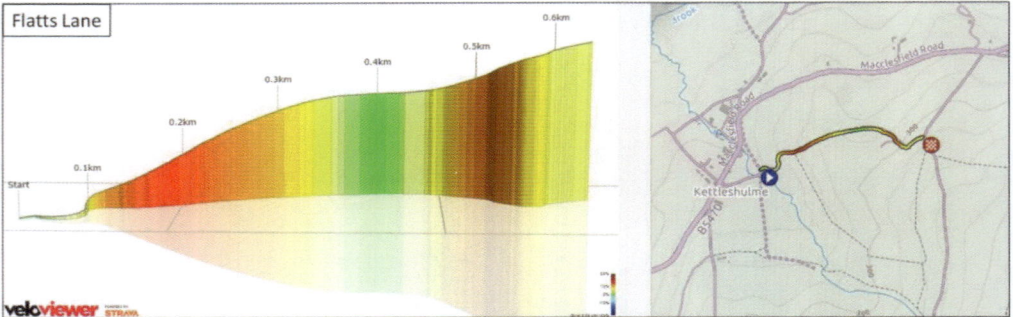

From the top, you descend Clayholes Road to the B5470 but turn immediately right to join Taxal Moor Road for a gentle climb along a quiet lane. A left turn then leads onto Whiteleas Road, which descends on tarmac initially but turns into a broken surface after the next bend as you head north to Taxal.

The route then turns right just before St. James' church to descend a very steep lane down to the River Goyt - there is a ford (photo), which is always deeper than it looks, or a footbridge if you'd rather keep your feet dry!

A short but steep gravel track then leads up to the A5004 for 2km of steady climbing before taking a right turn that leads down to Fernilee Reservoir.

The route then traverses the reservoir's dam and then follows a track that climbs (quite steeply) up to join a forest fire road.

The following 2km of the route follow the fire road (photo below) through the forest, with great views across the valley. At the end of the fire road, you descend The Street to ride alongside Errwood Reservoir.

From the southern end of Errwood reservor, you embark on the final climb of the route.

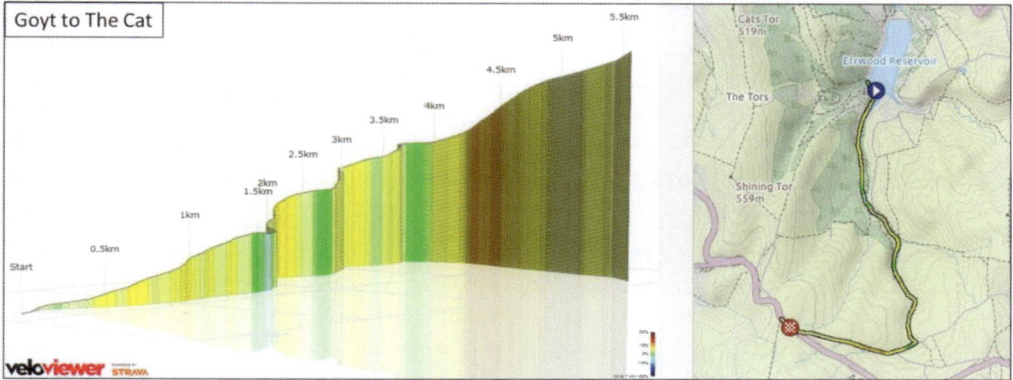

The climb starts with amazing scenery as you follow the River Goyt all the way upstream for 3.5km to reach Derbyshire Bridge. After crossing the cattle grid, you bear right and the gradient ramps up for a fairly punishing 1.5km all the way up to the landmark Cattle and Fiddle Inn. The next 3km section is on-road and downhill, with a blistering descent down to Wildboarclough - mind the bends. After you pass the Stanley Arms, you turn left and take a right turn for a sharp climb up towards Macclesfield Forest.

The final section of the route is a 3.5km trail through the southern side of the forest that is mainly down (but does have a couple of tricky sections of climb!)

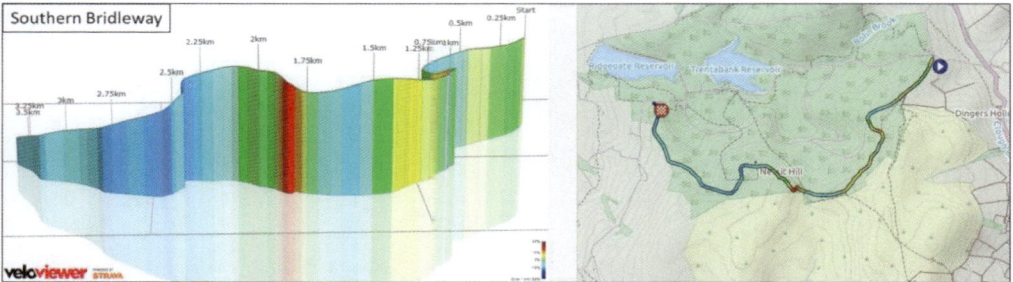

At its highest point, the trail rises clear of the trees to over 400m to provide fantastic views.

The final section of the trail is a steep and loose descent - ensure you come to a halt before reaching the gate at the end! Once through the gate, the route turns right and returns to the visitor centre.

13) CHESTER, CANALS AND CHEMICALS

Dist. (km)	Elev. (m)	m/km	BC Index	Miles	Feet	Terrain
87.4	742	8.5	64.9	54.3	2434	5

Route Start-point: Frodsham

Alternative Start-points: Delamere Forest, Kelsall, Chester, Neston, Ellesmere Port

Stop-off Options: Delamere Forest Visitor Centre, Citrus (Kelsall), Chester (lots), Net's Café (Ness)

Ideal Bike: Gravel bike (ok also on MTB)

The longest route in the book, this offers a great adventure that includes off-road sections around Foxhill, Delamere Forest, the Packhorse Bridges, the Shropshire Union Canal through the centre of Chester, the Chester Millennium Greenway, a boardwalk ride by the firing range onto the Wirral, the Wirral Way and a fascinating section through the chemical works by Frodsham Marsh.

The Low-down on the Climbs

The elevation profile for the route is illustrated in the diagram below, highlighting the key climbs.

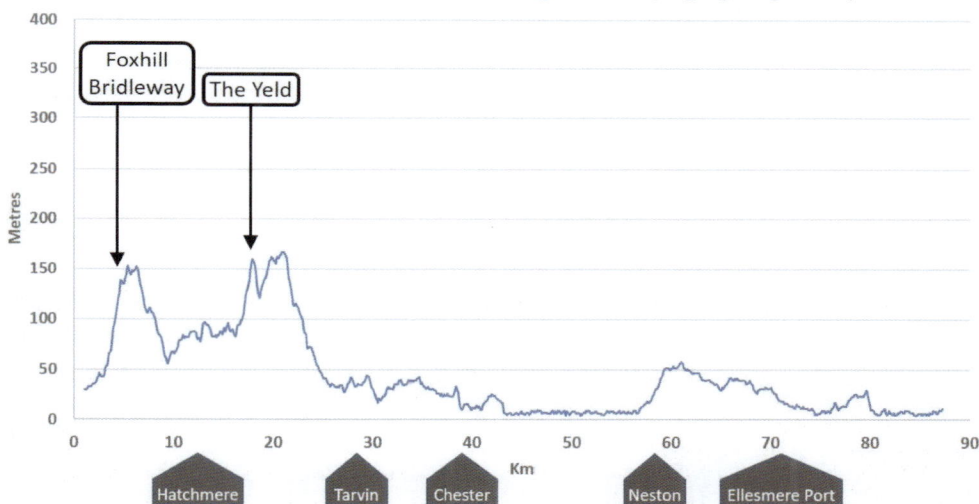

Climb	Distance (m)	Elevation Gain (m)	Peak Gradient	CBB Index	Features
Foxhill Bridleway	1000	57	10%	15.6	Stunning section through the trees
The Yeld	900	62	14%	18.9	Road climb that steepens gradually

Places of Interest on the Route

Tarvin Packhorse Bridges

Known also as "The Roman Bridges", these three narrow bridges trace their origins from the 14th century as part of the medieval road from London to Holyhead, forming a crossing over the River Gowy.

Chester Millennium Greenway

This is a tarmacked multi-user path that follows an old railway, it runs flat and smooth for 14km and takes you right through the middle of Chester without interruption.

CF Fertilisers

Established in 1965, this plant produces 1 million tonnes of nitrogen-based fertiliser each year.

Route Narrative

The route follows Route 5 for the initial kilometre before turning left onto Tarvin Road and then left again onto The Ridgeway to find the first off-road section, which includes the first notable climb of the route.

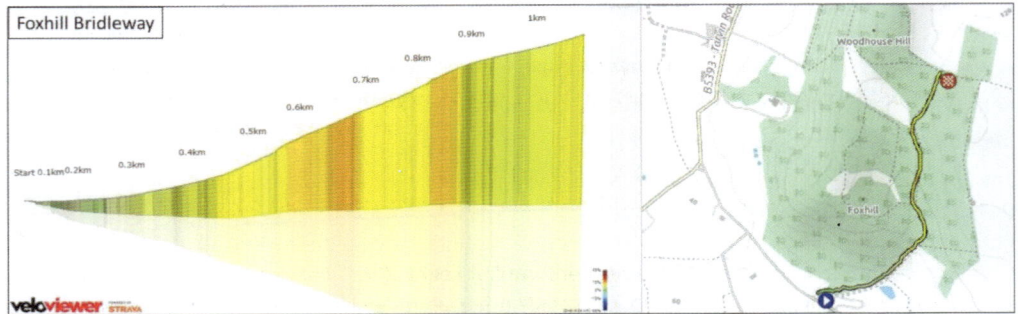

This bridleway follows the Sandstone Trail along the side of Foxhill, climbing all the way along a single-track path that is prone to muddy patches after wet weather. At a T-junction, the Sandstone Trail turns left but this route goes to the right and continues along a double-track lane, which leads to Dobers Lane.

You then descend along a series of lanes to reach the village of Kingsley to pick up a bumpy bridleway that takes you south and onto another bridleway that leads into the woods by Flaxmere and out to join Delamere Road. A right turn onto Ashton Road takes you into Delamere Forest and after 0.4km you take a left turn onto a waymarked cycle path for almost 4km of off-road forest trails (photo below).

As you emerge from the forest, you reach Yeld Lane for the only other notable climb of the ride.

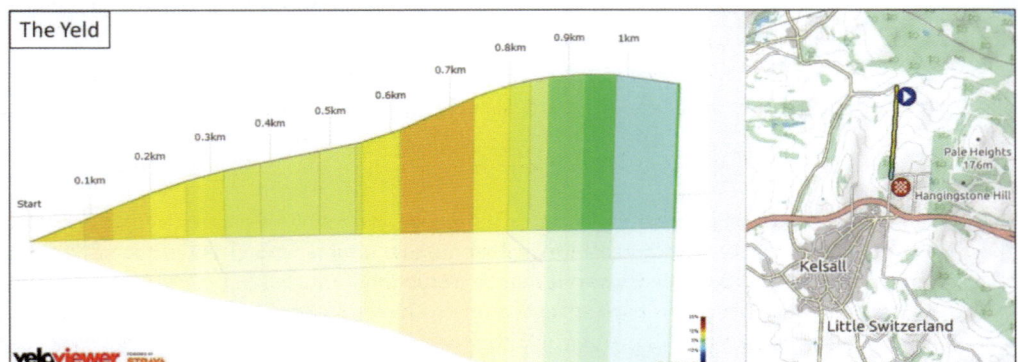

The climb follows a straight line and increases in gradient as you progress - with a pronounced ramp towards the top. Once over the top, the lane descends and crosses a bridge over the A54. You climb again onto the ridge and follow the winding lane to reach another bridleway that offers an exhilarating descent along a tight single-track path through the trees (photo below).

The route now joins Regional Cycle Route 71 for a great section of descent through Willington towards Tarvin. Just before you reach the Tarvin Bypass, you turn right and continue to follow Route 71 through residential streets to reach a crossing over the bypass. Hockenhull Lane now leads down through Hockenhull Platts and the Packhorse Bridges, with their tricky cobbled surfaces (see photo).

Route 71 still leads you on your way as you head west to reach Christleton, where you join the towpath of the Shropshire Union Canal to ride right into Chester City Centre. The towpath offers reasonably fast progress but be considerate with other users and take care around the bridges and locks.

After the canal makes a 90-degree turn, there is a spiral bridge to test your bike skills (photo below).

After passing the University, the route leaves the canal and joins the Chester Millennium Greenway, which offers a smooth and flat escape from the city and takes you over the Welsh border to cross a distinctive footbridge over the A494.

The Greenway leads you into Deeside Industrial Park to join Cycle Route 568, which takes you past the Sealand Rifle Range and back over the border. You then follow a fabulous boardwalk section over the marshes (photo below) to reach a brief section of tarmac on Station Road, before bearing left onto a narrow lane that leads past Net's Café (great place for a stop).

The lane continues past the café and becomes a gravel track that leads to the residential streets of Little Neston and onto the Wirral Way for more gravel (photo below).

You now follow the Cheshire Cycleway (Route 70) along a series of lanes through Little Sutton and Ellesmere Port to return back to the towpath of the Shropshire Union Canal - heading back towards Chester as far as the A5117 at Little Stanney. Route 5 now leads the way along the main road to Elton, where you turn left and follow a road around the perimeter of the Stanlow Refinery. The surface then changes from tarmac to gravel and you make your way towards the CF Fertilisers plant.

The following 5km are quite surreal as you ride past the Nitric Acid works on one side and the wind turbines on the other (photo below), after which you become aware of the busy M56 to your right whilst you continue away from the rush on the gravel lane.

At the end of the gravel track, you return to tarmac to cross over the motorway and arrive back into Frodsham.

ROUTE SUMMARY AND DOWNLOAD LINKS

The table below provides a summary of the routes and links to the .gpx files.

(take care if you are typing the links - some of the files have a double-underscore in the filename - sorry!)

Route	Dist. (km)	Elev. (m)	m/km	Download Links
Lyme Park and the Middlewood Way	36.1	506	14.0	https://ukcycleroutes.com/g-middlewood-lyme/
A pinch of salt	51.6	364	7.1	https://ukcycleroutes.com/g-malkins-bank/
Chelford Quarry and Marton Bridleways	48.2	439	9.1	https://ukcycleroutes.com/g-chelford-tidnock/
Delamere Forest Delight	49.8	435	8.7	https://ukcycleroutes.com/g-weaver-delamere/
Laureen's Ride	60.9	418	6.9	https://ukcycleroutes.com/g-double-laureen/
Mersey Paradise	64.7	458	7.1	https://ukcycleroutes.com/g-mersey-middlewood/
Biddulph Valley Way, Rudyard and Bosley Cloud	50.6	631	12.5	https://ukcycleroutes.com/g-biddulph-rudyard/
Cown Edge and The Peak Forest Canal	43.5	806	18.5	https://ukcycleroutes.com/g-cown-peak-forest/
Chewing Gravel	39.3	976	24.8	https://ukcycleroutes.com/g-stalybridge-chew/
Nantwich Canal-fest	74.4	519	7.0	https://ukcycleroutes.com/g-nantwich-middlewich/
Tatton Park and the TPT to Runcorn	84.2	636	7.6	https://ukcycleroutes.com/g-tatton-runcorn/
Macc Forest Monster	49.3	1302	26.4	https://ukcycleroutes.com/g-macc-forest-goyt/
Chester, Canals and Chemicals	87.4	742	8.5	https://ukcycleroutes.com/g-frodsham-chester/

How to Use the Download link

Each route has a download link, this will enable you to download a .gpx file to your local device (e.g. PC or phone).

You will then need to determine the required format of file for your navigation device. Newer devices (e.g. Garmin Edge 520 Plus, 530 and 800 series) will accept a .gpx file directly. Others will require an interim file conversion stage, for example:

- Older Garmin Edge 500 series work best with a .tcx file
- Garmin Edge 25 devices require a .fit file

There are numerous websites available that will perform the conversion for you, such as: https://www.gpsies.com/convert.do